James Fuller is a chancery barrister practising from Guildhall Chambers. James regularly appears in the High Court, County Court, Upper Tribunal (Lands Chamber), and First-tier Tribunal (Property Chamber). James is ranked in the Legal 500 as Tier 1 in Agriculture and Tier 2 in Property and Construction, and in Chambers & Partners as Band 2 in Agriculture & Rural Affairs and Up and Coming in Chancery.

Ollie Murrell is a chancery barrister practising from Guildhall Chambers. Ollie's practice spans chancery and real estate matters, with a particular focus on contentious trusts and estates matters. Ollie predominantly appears in the Chancery and Family Divisions of the High Court. Ollie recently acted as sole counsel in the seminal will formality case *Packer v Packer* [2025] EWHC 461 (Ch) in the High Court and Court of Appeal.

A Practical Guide to Missing Persons and the Administration of Estates

A Practical Guide to Missing Persons and the Administration of Estates

James Fuller
LL.B. (Hons), LL.M. (Bris), M.St. (Cantab)
Barrister of Lincoln's Inn
Guildhall Chambers

Ollie Murrell
LL.B. (Hons), LL.M.
Barrister of Lincoln's Inn
Guildhall Chambers

Law Brief Publishing

Published 2026 by Law Brief Publishing, an imprint of Law Brief Publishing Ltd
30 The Parks
Minehead
Somerset
TA24 8BT

www.lawbriefpublishing.com

Paperback: 978-1-918241-12-9

For all missing persons

FOREWORD

By His Honour Judge Paul Matthews

Most of our legal system is concerned with allegations of facts, disputes about things that are said to have happened, or sometimes not to have happened. Two people have made a contract, and one of them says that the other one has not performed its side of the bargain. Two neighbours argue about the position of the boundary between their properties. One says that it lies along this line, the other that it lies along that. A baby has been injured. The local authority points that finger at the parents. They deny it, or perhaps one of them accuses the other.

These disputes resolve uncertainty between two or more people who wish to dispute it. This is adversarial law at its best. But, very occasionally, the law needs to concern itself with two logically prior problems, arising from uncertainty where there is as yet no-one to dispute it. There are two stages in this kind of uncertainty. The second of them is what the process is to resolve the uncertainty in the absence of a disputant. The first, of course, is what to do in the interim, before any process can be gone through to resolve the uncertainty.

Nowhere is this clearer than the law's response to a person who goes missing. The problem is that missing persons have both rights and duties. Specifically, they may own property, such as homes, bank accounts, and motor cars, and be involved in financial transactions, contracts, insurance policies, pensions, and so on. All these usually need to be looked after, even in that person's absence. Moreover, everyone knows that, if that person has in fact died, other people will become involved, whether as personal representatives of the deceased's estate or as beneficiaries of the assets in question. The ultimate decision-maker will at that point change.

English law has long had rules enabling a process of presumption of death to be undertaken in respect of a missing person. It also has rules enabling the appointment of a person to manage a person's property when that person is unable to do so. The modern law on this subject is stated in the Guardianship (Missing Persons) Act 2017 and the Presumption of Death Act 2013. These two Acts, together with some secondary legislation, provide a sound statutory basis for presuming the death of missing persons, and for safeguarding their assets before that can be done.

But it is one thing to have laws. It is another to implement them effectively. The cases that they are intended to deal with are not numerous. Few judges will ever gain much experience of them, and even fewer lawyers will ever be asked to deal with them. In any event, many people today coming into contact with the law take the view that they cannot afford to consult a lawyer and they try to engage with the legal process themselves. Usually, they are wrong about this, and it is a bad idea for everyone concerned, but especially for the litigants in person. But that is another story.

The problem here is this. If the court is going to give someone the right to deal with property that hitherto was entirely under the control of a person who now cannot be found, or at least contacted, then the law must build in safeguards against abuse, fraud, or worse. But that creates the need for checks, extra formality, indeed bureaucracy, and this at a time when (in most cases) those who care for the missing person are really hurting. That makes the law complicated, and it looks brutal. Litigants in person (obviously) find it even more difficult. Ouch.

What judges, lawyers and litigants in person need is a book which explains in simple terms how these laws work, and how they interact with the other processes which already exist in English law, and which perform the same or similar functions. This book, written by two very able (though, in my eyes at least, still young) barristers is what they need. It is written in clear terms, though without loss of detail, and covers the ground admirably. The target audiences do not need to read this book. But they will be better off if they do. I commend it to them.

Paul Matthews
Bristol Civil and Family Justice Centre
September 2025

PREFACE

Missing persons leave behind not only their own estates, but also the estates in which they have an interest. The law and procedure relating to the estate and affairs of a missing person is complex, and the subject matter is tragic.

The civil law relating to missing persons can arise in a number of a different contexts, and for this reason commentary and guidance on this area of law is currently dispersed throughout various practitioner texts, which address numerous other unrelated issues. The aim of this book is to change that and to provide, for the first time, a comprehensive practical guide to a subject which, as far as the author's understand, has never been dealt with comprehensively in one book before. This book takes the reader through the relevant legal principles using clear and simple language, including all the latest developments and case law. It provides a step-by-step guide through the applications required, as well as the practical steps to take before and after making an application. The authors hope that this book will prove a helpful guide through the troubled waters of the law of missing persons, for anyone who finds themselves dealing with the estate of a missing person or involving a missing person.

The authors would like to thank His Honour Judge Paul Matthews, and Zachariah Pullar of Guildhall Chambers, for their helpful comments on an earlier draft. All opinions, omissions, oversights, and errors, remain the authors' own.

This book aims to state the law and procedure of England and Wales as of 1 October 2025.

James Fuller & Ollie Murrell
November 2025

CONTENTS

CHAPTER ONE

INTRODUCTION

A. Missing people

Dealing with and administering estates of or involving a missing person is not something that many trusts and estates practitioners will be familiar with. Aside from a handful of people, many will never think about missing people beyond the occasional news report, or the sensationalist books and television documentaries about public figures who have disappeared (e.g. Lord Lucan,[1] Richey Edwards of the Manic Street Preachers, and Grand Duchess Anastasia Romanov). Whilst the concept of a "missing person" may seem an unusual one to most, sadly people go missing, or cannot be traced, more than one would think. According to the statistics of the charity Missing People, in the United Kingdom there are nearly 350,000 reported missing incidents every year, over 170,000 people are reported missing every year, and someone is reported missing every 90 seconds.[2] Despite globalism, the advent of the internet and social media and increased monitoring of individuals, it is sadly still often impossible, or – as will be discussed – impractical, to trace individuals.

B. Development of the law

In the 1700s and 1800s, the Courts of England and Wales were often called upon to deal with the estates of missing people. During this period, it was not uncommon for individuals, sometimes accompanied by their

---

1 Richard John Bingham, 7th Earl of Lucan

2 'Key Information' (*Missing People*) <https://www.missingpeople.org.uk/for-professionals/policy-and-research/information-and-research/key-information> accessed 14 October 2025

families, to leave England and Wales (as well as other parts of the United Kingdom) to take up posts in the colonies, dominions, mandates, protectorates, and other territories ruled or administered by the United Kingdom and its predecessor states. Similarly, the British Army and the East India Company would send those within its employ all over the world. A further category of person who would travel the world during this time were simply those doing so for personal reasons, such as tourism, leisure, exploration, adventure, or even in pursuit of riches. If any of these individuals failed to return, they would leave behind estates which required administration and create estates with missing beneficiaries. Those interested in such estates – in most cases, personal representatives or creditors – called on the Courts of Chancery, and subsequently the Chancery Division of the High Court, to seek directions.

A line of authorities emerged in the 1800s with two distinct functions: (i) to raise a presumption of death; and (ii) to permit personal representatives to distribute the estate on the basis a beneficiary had died at some prior point.[3] Parliament has now intervened. The enactment of the Presumption of Death Act 2013 ("**PDA 2013**") has, for the most part, replaced the common law presumption of death principles and it is no longer possible to apply for a declaration of presumed death under legislation enacted prior to the PDA 2013 *if* that declaration can be made pursuant to the PDA 2013. The PDA 2013 has also diminished the scope of what became known as the "Benjamin Order" for missing beneficiaries. The introduction of the Guardianship (Missing Persons)

---

3 The detail of those cases and historical position is beyond the scope of this work. Should the reader be interested to read further in respect of the historical position then please see: *Prudential Assurance Co v Edmonds* (1877) 2 App Cas 487, HL; *Wills v Palmer* (1904) 53 WR 169; *Re Bowden* (1904) 21 TLR 13; *Lal Chand Marwari v Mahant Ramrup Gir* (1925) 42 TLR 159, PC; *Chard v Chard* [1956] P 259, [1955] 3 All ER 721; *Bullock v Bullock* [1960] 2 All ER 307, [1960] 1 WLR 975, DC; *Bayes-Walker v Bayes-Walker* [2010] EWHC 3142 (Ch), [2011] WTLR 1143

Act 2017 ("**G(MP)A 2017**") has provided a further framework to enable a guardian to manage the property and financial affairs of a missing person.

Nevertheless, the statutory framework and the common law remains uncharted territory to many, and the guidance from practitioner texts and case law is understandably limited. However, when a person goes missing or cannot be traced, there will come a time when their estate and the estates of which they are beneficiaries must be managed and/or administered.

C. This Book

In the following chapters, this book will consider the implications of missing or untraceable people and the resolution of those implications in the context of estates, probate, and inheritance.

There are two types of cases addressed in this book. The first regards the estate of the missing person. This first type of case has readily obvious difficulties. There will usually be a house, bank accounts, and other assets in their name, and something needs to be done to manage or administer those assets. The second type of case regards the estates of others in which the missing person has an interest. The second type of cases usually, but not always, involves personal representatives who are unsure how to deal with the interest of a missing beneficiary and who, if anyone, should take it in their place.

Readers should note that not every chapter will apply to both types of cases. Whilst some are cross-applicable, other chapters specifically regard one type of case.

D. Definitions

As there is duplication of many terms, and some have specialist definitions, in addition to those terms defined above, this book adopts the following defined terms:

- "**AEA 1925**": Administration of Estates Act 1925;
- "**Chancery Guide**": *Business and Property Courts of England and Wales Chancery Guide 2022* (Fifth Update, September 2025);
- "**CPA 2004**": Civil Partnership Act 2004;
- "**CPFO 2008**": Civil Proceedings Fees Order 2008 (SI 2008/1053);
- "**CPR**": Civil Procedure Rules 1998 (SI 1998/3132);
- "**Deceased**": the person, not being the missing person, in respect of whose estate is the subject of the application, claim or administration;
- "**FPFO 2008**": Family Proceedings Fees Order 2008 (SI 2008/1054);
- "**FPR**": Family Procedure Rules 2010 (SI 2010/2955);
- "**Missing person**": a person who is missing or cannot be traced – this term, as defined here, does not mean missing person within the meaning of s.1 of the G(MP)A 2017 or s.20 of the PDA 2013;
- "**MCA 2015**": Mental Capacity Act 2005;
- "**N-CPR 1987**": Non-Contentious Probate Rules 1987/2004;
- "**Personal representatives**": unless otherwise stated this has the following meaning as set out at s.55(xi) of the AEA 1925:

  > "'Personal representative' means the executor, original or by representation, or administrator for the time being

of a deceased person, and as regards any liability for the payment of death duties includes any person who takes possession of or intermeddles with the property of a deceased person without the authority of the personal representatives or the Court, and 'executor' includes a person deemed to be appointed executor as respects settled land";

- "**SCA 1981**": Senior Courts Act 1981;

- "**TA 1925**": Trustees Act 1925;

- "**Type 1 Case**": a case regarding the missing person's own estate; and

- "**Type 2 Case**": a case regarding the estate of another in which the missing person has an interest as a beneficiary, creditor, personal representative or generally.

This book also refers from time to time to the following practitioner texts:

- *Lewin on Trusts* (1st supp, 20th edn, Sweet & Maxwell 2023) ("***Lewin***"); and

- *Williams, Mortimer & Sunnucks – Executors, Administrators and Probate* (22nd edn, Sweet & Maxwell 2023) ("***Williams, Mortimer & Sunnucks***").

References to numbers when referring to the above works, or to any cases referred to in this book, are to the paragraph numbers of the works and cases referred to. All references to legislation are to the amended versions as of 1 October 2025, unless otherwise stated.

PART ONE

PRELIMINARY CONSIDERATIONS

CHAPTER TWO

ADVERTISEMENT

As a precursor to any application regarding a missing person in both Type 1 Cases and Type 2 Cases, the personal representatives must advertise for the missing person to come forward. This can take many forms, but it is important to note general advertisement is distinct from statutory advertisement for creditors under s.27 of the TA 1925. Unlike under s.27, personal representatives will not obtain protection from liability if they distribute after advertisement in respect of missing testators or beneficiaries.

Save for applications under the PDA 2013 and G(MP)A 2017,[4] there is no requirement for personal representatives to comply with s.27 or advertise. Nonetheless, the Court will expect some form of advertisement to be carried out before other orders are made, save in exceptional circumstances. A modified version of s.27 is a useful starting point; the personal representatives should give notice of:

- The name and last known circumstances of the missing person;
- Details of the estate and their intention to distribute the estate;
- Require the missing person to get in touch with the personal representatives and provide evidence they are the missing person; and
- State the time in which no action will be taken. Section 27 requires no less than two months of advertisement. The time will

4 See Chapter 4, Section F(f) and Chapter 6, Section G(e), respectively

vary on the level of certainty as to the missing person's circumstances and the value of their share.

The notice should be placed in:

- The London Gazette;
- In a local newspaper in circulation in any place where the missing person was known to have lived or visited;
- In "*such other like notice including notices elsewhere than in England and Wales as would...have been directed by a Court of competent jurisdiction in an action for administration*" (s.27(1), TA 1925). Typical examples may include a local parish newsletter or a group magazine; and
- On the internet, such as on social media or forums.

If the missing person was known to reside abroad, the same process should be repeated in the relevant country. However, the personal representative's duty to advertise abroad extends further: "*If...there be any reasonable ground for supposing that there is a claimant residing in a foreign country or in one of our colonies, the notice should be advertised there also*".[5] Special provisions exist in respect of foreign nationals who are resident in certain countries; see Chapter 8, Section E.

Once the prescribed time has expired without answer, the personal representatives will need to make an application to the Court subject to the possible alternative of insurance.

5 *Newton v Sherry* (1875-76) L.R. 1 C.P.D. 246 at 256

CHAPTER THREE

INSURANCE

It is now settled that an indemnity insurance policy can generally be substituted for the relevant Court order in Type 2 Cases (only), particularly where the estate or the missing person's share is modest in value. Richard McCombe QC (as he then was) sitting as a Deputy High Court Judge gave the following advice in *Re Evans* [1999] 2 All ER 777 at 785-786:

> "[I]n small intestate administrations, where frequently the representative will have a personal interest, sizeable sums should not have to be tied up indefinitely for fear of the re-emergence of a long lost beneficiary. The missing beneficiary policy does provide, at relatively small cost, a practical answer to such problems."

Richard McCombe QC further held in *Re Evans* that the costs of the insurance are properly chargeable to the estate pursuant to personal representatives' indemnity (at 786).

Missing person insurance policies can now be obtained at relatively limited cost,[6] although readers should be aware the cost of insurance has increased disproportionately in recent years. Nevertheless, as personal representatives can recover the cost of the policy from the estate, it is recommended that personal representatives obtain cover for the entirety of a missing person's estate (or share in it) plus interest. Otherwise, the personal representative may find themselves liable for any shortfall. This

6 If insurance is sought in respect of larger and/or complex estates, particularly where trust or company structures will be affected, bespoke insurance policies will likely be required. In such cases, it may be appropriate to seek advice from a specialist broker or insurer

possibility was hinted at by Mr McCombe QC in *Re Evans* at 788, a case in which the missing person reappeared and claimed both their share and interest (which was, by that point, relatively substantial).

Fortunately for the personal representative in *Re Evans*, the Court exercised its power under s.61 of the TA 1925 to relieve the personal representative of liability for interest. Mr McCombe QC's judgment on that issue hinged in large part on the personal representative having acted on legal advice premised on all the facts the personal representative reasonably could ascertain and, as required by s.61, lacked any dishonesty.

It is hoped that personal representatives would satisfy the non-dishonesty requirement; the reasonableness of steps taken is highly subjective. Judicial determinations of reasonableness are inherently unpredictable and difficult to challenge on appeal. *Re Evans* highlights the need for an insurance policy not just to cover the missing persons share in full, but also any interest which may accrue on the share for an indeterminable amount of time. This latter factor will invariably cause an insurance policy to cost more than otherwise it would.

As the Courts have given broad support to the use of insurance policies, particularly in small and modest estates, a personal representative who obtains a more expensive policy to insure both the lump sum entitlement and interest is unlikely to be criticised.

Where an insurance policy is significantly less expensive than a Court application, and the estate/share is modest, insurance will usually be the preferable option and, if anything, will provide greater protection for personal representatives and beneficiaries. If the costs are broadly comparable, a *Benjamin Order* may be the safer option for the personal representative. The recipient beneficiaries may need to consider obtaining their own insurance policy on receipt of the missing persons share to protect themselves from the risks of the missing person resurfacing.

PART TWO

APPLICATIONS

CHAPTER FOUR

DECLARATIONS OF PRESUMED DEATH UNDER THE PDA 2013

A. Background

The enactment of the PDA 2013 on 1 October 2014 has introduced a relatively swift and straightforward procedure that allows a missing person's spouse, civil partner, parent, child, sibling, or any person that the Court considers to have a "sufficient interest" in the determination of the application, to apply to the Court under s.1 of the PDA 2013 for a declaration of presumed death where a person who is missing is either (i) thought to have died, or (ii) has not been known to be alive for a period of at least seven years.[7]

Williams, Mortimer & Sunnucks explains at 54-56:

> "Ordinarily, an application will be made so that the process for obtaining a grant can begin; this will, of course, be before administration of the estate has begun and there will be no need for the involvement of a personal representative, unless the missing person has left no relative to make an application. A declaration under the 2013 Act will, however, be effective against all persons and for all purposes, including for the purposes of the acquisition of an interest in any property, and, when making the declaration, the court will

[7] PDA 2013, s.1(1)

> have power to determine questions relating to interests in property arising as a result of the declaration."

If an application for a declaration of presumed death is made, the Court *must* make a declaration of presumed death if it is satisfied that a missing person has either (i) died, or (ii) not been known to be alive for at least seven years.[8] A declaration made by the Court will be conclusive evidence of the missing person's presumed death, as well as the date and time of their presumed death.[9]

Following the making of a declaration of presumed death, an application can be made to the General Registry Office for a certificate of presumed death, which is akin to a death certificate, and will allow the personal representative(s) to deal with the property and affairs of the missing person in the same way as if that missing person had actually died and a death certificate was issued in the usual way.[10]

A declaration made under the PDA 2013 can be varied or revoked by what is known as a "*variation order*".[11] An application for a variation order can be made by a missing person's spouse, civil partner, parent, child, sibling, or any person that the Court considers has sufficient interest in the determination of the application.[12] The Explanatory Notes to the PDA 2013 at 24 explain that an "*obvious example*" of circumstances in which it would be appropriate to seek a variation order is: *"where the missing person returns, still alive; or where there is clear evidence of the missing person having been alive at a time later than that declared as the time of death in the original declaration."*

---

8 PDA 2013, s.2(1)

9 PDA 2013, s3(1)

10 PDA 2013, s.3

11 PDA 2013, s.5(1)

12 PDA 2013, s.5(2)

This chapter is predominantly concerned with how to prepare an application for a declaration of presumed death, but reference is also made (although not in detail) to applications for a variation order.

A declaration of presumed death is necessary in Type 1 Cases, but may also be appropriate in Type 2 Cases. In most standard Type 2 Cases, the personal representative will also be a person who can apply under the PDA 2013. In those cases, the PDA 2013 procedure can be used for dual purposes. However, the PDA 2013 will not assist where (i) the personal representative does not have a sufficient interest under the PDA 2013, (ii) the time/date of death is uncertain and the missing person is required to have died before or after a certain point, or (iii) it appears the missing person is merely untraceable as opposed to dead/not thought to be alive. Therefore, the Benjamin Order still remains the primary tool in Type 2 Cases.

B. JURISDICTION

The Court's jurisdiction to hear and determine an application for a declaration of presumed death only arises if:

1. the missing person was domiciled in England and Wales on the day on which he or she was last known to be alive;[13]

2. the missing person had been habitually resident in England and Wales throughout the period of one year ending with that day;[14] or

3. if the application is made by a spouse of civil partner of the missing person;

[13] PDA 2013, s.1(3)(a)

[14] PDA 2013, s.1(3)(b)

a. the applicant is domiciled in England and Wales on the day on which the application is made;[15] or

b. the applicant has been habitually resident in England and Wales throughout the period of one year ending with that day.[16]

If an applicant cannot satisfy/prove the above to the Court, then an application under the PDA 2013 will fail for lack of jurisdiction, and the issue fee (see Subsection F(d) below), and any other costs incurred, will be wasted.[17]

C. Circumstances in which the Court will make a declaration

The effect of ss.1(1)-(2) is that an application can be made to the Court for a declaration that a missing person is presumed to be dead where that person is either (i) thought to have died, or (ii) has not been known to be alive for a period of at least seven years.

Section 2(1) provides that the Court *must* make a declaration of presumed death if it is satisfied that the missing person has (i) died, or (ii) not been known to be alive for at least seven years. The Court must be satisfied that it can make a declaration on the balance of probabilities (see Subsection F(g) below).

---

15 PDA 2013, s.1(4)(a)

16 PDA 2013, s.1(5)(a) and s.1(4)(b)

17 For an example of an application that failed due to the Court lacking jurisdiction, please see *Reynolds v Saul* [2024] EWHC 3593 (Ch)

D. POWERS

The PDA 2013 provides the Court with the following powers:

1. to make a declaration of presumed death;[18]

2. to determine any question which relates to an interest in property;[19]

3. to determine the domicile of the missing person at the time of his or her presumed death;[20]

4. to make such order as it considers reasonable in relation to any interest in property acquired as a result of a declaration;[21]

5. to direct that the value of any interest in property acquired as a result of the declaration is not to be recoverable by virtue of a variation order;[22]

6. to direct that the value of any interest in property acquired as a result of the declaration is not to be recoverable (i) in any circumstances, or (ii) where conditions specified in the order are met;[23]

7. to vary or revoke or revoke a declaration;[24]

---

18 PDA 2013, s.2(1)

19 PDA 2013, s.4(1)(a) and s.7(a)

20 PDA 2013, s.4(1)(b) and s.7(b)

21 PDA 2013, s.4(2)

22 PDA 2013, s.4(3)

23 PDA 2013, s.4(4)

24 PDA 2013, s.5(1)

8. when making a variation order, to make such further order (if any) as it considers reasonable in relation to any interest in property acquired as a result of the declaration varied or revoked by the order;[25]

9. at any stage to direct that papers relating to an application for a declaration or variation order be sent to the Attorney General;[26]

10. where the Attorney General incurs costs in connection with an application for a declaration or a variation order, to make such order as the Court considers appropriate as to the payment of the costs by parties to the proceedings;[27]

11. to require a person who is not a party to proceedings to provide the Court with specified information it considers relevant to the question of whether the missing person is dead or alive;[28] and

12. to direct the trustee of a trust affected by a declaration to take out an insurance policy in respect of any claim which may arise by virtue of an order to vary or revoke a declaration.[29]

E. CLAIMANTS

Although s.1(2) provides that any person may apply to the Court for a declaration of presumed death, this is caveated by s.1(5) which provides that the Court must refuse to hear an application for a declaration of presumed death unless the applicant is either:

---

25 PDA 2013, s.7(2)

26 PDA 2013, s.10(1)

27 PDA 2013, s.10(3)

28 PDA 2013, s.12

29 PDA 2013, s.13(1)

1. the missing person's spouse, civil partner, parent, child, or sibling (which includes half-blood siblings);[30] or

2. someone that the Court considers as having "sufficient interest" in the determination of the application.[31]

The term "sufficient interest" is not defined in the PDA 2013, although recent case law has provided guidance on the types of individuals that *may* have sufficient interest.

In *Re P (Presumption of Death)* [2021] EWHC 3099 (Fam), Poole J observed at [7] that, although a long-term cohabitee is not automatically deemed to have sufficient interest to bring a claim, "*[a] long-term cohabitee might be as close as anyone to the subject person.*" Long-term cohabitee applicants must make sure, however, that they evidence their reasons and interest in applying for a declaration of presumed death thoroughly in their witness statement/evidence in support of the application as they must still convince the Court that they have sufficient interest in the determination of the application (see Subsection F(g) below for further information).

In *Re Fisher* [2023] EWHC 979 (Ch), HHJ Paul Matthews (sitting as a Judge of the High Court) at [22] found that a person who intends to prove a testamentary paper (i.e. an executor who seeks to prove a will) does have sufficient interest in applying for a declaration of presumed death even though the paper has not yet been proved.

HHJ Matthews in *Re Fisher* at [9] identified the following categories of individuals who *may* have an interest in a Court declaring that a person is presumed dead:

30 PDA 2013, s.1(5)(a) and s.20(1)

31 PDA 2013, s.1(5)(b)

> "One is the very real emotional interest that members of a family, and indeed close friends, have in each other's lives simply as such. Some of those family members (though by no means all) are covered by section 1(5)(a), but others are not. A second is the financial interest that some people have in the continued lives of others, such as minors living with the missing person and indeed other dependants. A third is the financial interest that some have in the deaths of others, such as heirs, beneficiaries under insurance policies and the like. A fourth interest is that of the public itself, in relation to aspects of government such as civil registration, taxation and social security. There may be other interests too."

Continuing at [10], HHJ Matthews said: *"How far the term 'sufficient interest' in the 2013 Act extends to these various interests, and indeed others, is a matter which should be decided on the usual casuistic basis."*

In *Reynolds v Saul* [2024] EWHC 3593 (Ch), a deceased person's estate was held to have a real and substantial interest in whether a missing person was presumed to have died and when that happened. Applying *Re Fisher*, the Court held that the personal representative of the deceased's estate (who was the claimant) was deemed to have sufficient interest in the determination of the application (although the application was refused on other grounds).

For those reasons set out above (and set out below at Subsection F(g)), an applicant who considers themselves to have sufficient interest should set out in the claim form and/or any supporting witness statement the circumstances as to why they believe they have sufficient interest to apply for a declaration of presumed death.

F. MAKING AN APPLICATION

(a) Rules, procedure, and venue

The rules and procedure for making an application are set out in the PDA 2013, Part V of CPR 57 (rr.57.17-57.23), and Practice Direction 57B.

The authors stress the importance of reading the procedural requirements and making sure that they have been complied with. PDA 2013 applications are highly procedural and overlooking any steps will result in delays in determination. Should an applicant fail to comply with a procedural requirement (e.g. by advertising the claim within the prescribed time limit), then the applicant should consider, if they consider there is good reason for the failure, seeking relief pursuant to CPR r.3.1(2)(a), which grants the Court general powers of management to extend the time for compliance with any rule, practice direction or Court order.

Proceedings must be issued in the High Court[32] and in either the Chancery Division or the Family Division.[33]

The CPR applies to proceedings under the PDA 2013 which are issued in the Family Division, except that the provisions of the FPR relating to the drawing up and service of orders apply instead of the provisions in Part 40 of the CPR and Practice Direction 40B.[34]

---

32 PDA 2013, s.1(2); CPR r.57.18(2)

33 CPR r.57.18(1)(a)-(b)

34 CPR r.57.18(2)

(b) Claim Form

A claim for a declaration of presumed death (or for a variation order) must be made by issuing a Claim Form in accordance with Part 8 of the CPR.[35]

The Claim Form must:

1. be in Form N208;[36]

2. state that Part 8 of the CPR applies;[37]

3. contain a brief outline of the facts;

4. state the question which the applicant/claimant wants the Court to decide (i.e. that the Court is being asked to make a declaration of presumed death);[38]

5. the remedy sought and the legal basis for the claim to that remedy (i.e. a declaration of presumed death on the basis that the Court is satisfied that a missing person has died or has not been known to be alive for at least seven years);[39]

6. that the claim is made under the PDA 2013;[40]

---

35 CPR r.57.19(1)

36 Form N208 is available at <https://www.gov.uk/government/publications/form-n208-claim-form-cpr-part-8> accessed 14 October 2025

37 CPR r.8.2(a)

38 CPR r.8.2(b)(i)

39 CPR r.8.2(b)(ii)

40 CPR r.8.2(c)

7. if the claimant is claiming in a representative capacity, what that capacity is;[41]

8. if the defendant is sued in a representative capacity, what that capacity is[42] (although it should be noted that it is considered inappropriate to otherwise join any person as a defendant to an application and in *Greathead v Greathead* [2017] EWHC 1154 (Ch), HHJ Paul Matthews (sitting as a Judge of the High Court) suggested at [7] that *"[t]he sensible course is for the claimant not to name any defendant, and the case to be known simply by the name of the claimant and the name of the missing person, such as '[NAME], claimant, in the matter of [name of missing person]'"*);

9. include or be accompanied by a witness statement setting out the following information (where known) required by Paragraph 1.1. of Practice Direction 57B:

    a. information about the claimant:

        i. the claimant's name and address;[43]

        ii. the claimant's relationship to the missing person;[44]

        iii. if the claimant is not the missing person's spouse, civil partner, parent, child or sibling, details of the claimant's interest in the determination of the application;[45] and

---

41 CPR r.8.2(d)

42 CPR r.8.2(e)

43 CPR PD 57B, para 1.1(1)(a)

44 CPR PD 57B, para 1.1(1)(b)

45 CPR PD 57B, para 1.1(1)(c)

b. information about the missing person:

i. the missing person's name and surname, and any other names by which the missing person is or has formerly been known;[46]

ii. the missing person's gender;[47]

iii. the missing person's maiden surname (if any);[48]

iv. the missing person's date and place of birth;[49]

v. the occupation of the missing person;[50]

vi. the occupation, name and surname of (i) the missing person's spouse or civil partner (or late spouse or civil partner if the marriage or civil partnership ended on death),[51] or (ii) where the missing person was under 16 years of age, the missing person's parents;[52]

vii. the missing person's National Insurance number;[53]

---

46 CPR PD 57B, para 1.1(2)(a)

47 CPR PD 57B, para 1.1(2)(b)

48 CPR PD 57B, para 1.1(2)(c)

49 CPR PD 57B, para 1.1(2)(d)

50 CPR PD 57B, para 1.1(2)(e)

51 CPR PD 57B, para 1.1(2)(f)(i)

52 CPR PD 57B, para 1.1(2)(f)(ii)

53 CPR PD 57B, para 1.1(2)(g)

   viii. the date on which missing person is thought to have died, or on which the missing person was last known to have been alive;[54]

   ix. on which of the grounds in s.1(4) of the PDA 2013 the Court is considered to have jurisdiction to entertain the claim;[55]

   x. the usual or last known address of the missing person;[56] and

   xi. the name and address of the spouse or civil partner, parents, children or siblings of the missing person (if any, and if not the claimant);[57]

c. information about steps taken to trace the missing person:

   i. details of any enquiries made, or other steps taken to trace the missing person or confirm when the missing person was last known to be alive;[58] and

   ii. details of the results of such enquiries or other steps;[59]

d. information about the missing person's property:

---

54 CPR PD 57B, para 1.1(2)(h)

55 CPR PD 57B, para 1.1(2)(i)

56 CPR PD 57B, para 1.1(2)(j)

57 CPR PD 57B, para 1.1(2)(k)

58 CPR PD 57B, para 1.1(3)(a)

59 CPR PD 57B, para 1.1(3)(b)

i. an estimate of the total value of the assets of the missing person;[60]

ii. details of property owned by the missing person;[61] and

iii. details of the interest of any other person in the missing person's property which it is sought to have determined by the Court;[62]

e. information about advertisement and receipts of the notice of the claim:

i. details of the newspaper in which the claimant proposes to advertise the claim;[63] and

ii. details of the persons to whom the claimant is giving notice of the claim and, where notice is being given to a person under CPR r.57.20(1)(f), the nature of that person's interest in the claim.[64]

Compliance with Paragraph 1.1 of Practice Direction 57B should be checked prior to issuing a claim/application as non-compliance can result in delays in the claim/application being heard and risks the claim/application being struck out.

The Chancery Guide at 23.35 provides that a draft order in Form CH42 should always be attached to the Claim Form, with Annex A completed

---

60 CPR PD 57B, para 1.1(4)(a)

61 CPR PD 57B, para 1.1(4)(b)

62 CPR PD 57B, para 1.1(4)(c)

63 CPR PD 57B, para 1.1(5)(a)

64 CPR PD 57B, para 1.1(5)(b)

(a Schedule of prescribed information for the General Register) which should satisfy the requirement of Practice Direction 57B in respect of the time of presumed death.[65] Form CH42 is useful and helps focus any application on the matters that the Court will be concerned with should an application be successful.

(c) Notice

Notice of the claim/application must be given to the following persons (where applicable) by serving a copy of the application within seven days of issuing the claim:[66]

1. the missing person's spouse or civil partner,[67] any parents,[68] any children[69] and any siblings (including half-blood siblings);[70] or

2. if there are none of the above, then the nearest relative of the missing person (if known to the claimant);[71] and

3. any other person (including in particular any insurance company) appearing to the claimant to have an interest in the claim.[72]

---

65 Form CH42 is available at <https://www.gov.uk/government/publications/form-ch42-presumption-of-death-act-2013> accessed 14 October 2025

66 PDA 2013, s.9(1); CPR 57.20(3)

67 CPR r.57.20(1)(a)

68 CPR r.57.20(1)(b)

69 CPR r.57.20(1)(c)

70 CPR r.57.20(1)(d)

71 CPR r.57.20(1)(e)

72 CPR r.57.20(1)(f)

(d) Issuing without notice

If a claim for a declaration of presumed death is made without naming a defendant (which, for those reasons set out above, it should be), CPR r.8.2A applies but in a form modified by CPR r.57.19(4), which provides that instead of "without naming a defendant" the rule has been modified to substitute this wording with "without serving notice on any person".

If an applicant considers that there is no person set out at of CPR r.57.20(1)(a)-(f) upon which they should serve notice, an application for permission to issue will need to be made and the applicant will need to explain why they believe that there is no such person.[73] An application for permission to issue should be made at the same time as the claim is issued and supported by evidence.[74]

(e) Issue Fee

The issue fee will be:

- £646 if filed in the Chancery Division;[75] or
- £279 if filed in the Family Division.[76]

(f) Advertisement

The claimant must, within seven days of the issue of the claim, ensure that the notice of the claim is published:[77]

---

[73] CPR r.57.19(4); Practice Direction 57B, paragraph 1.3.

[74] *Chancery Guide*, paragraph 23.34

[75] CPFO, Schedule 1, fee 1.5

[76] FPFO 2008, Schedule 1, fee 1.1

[77] PDA 2013, s.9(2); CPR r.57.21(1)

1. in a form which meets the requirements set out in Practice Direction 57B;[78] and

2. in at least one newspaper circulating in the vicinity of the last known address of the missing person.[79]

Paragraph 2.1 of Practice Direction 57B provides that the advertisement of the claim must be in the form set out at Paragraph 2.1 of Practice Direction 57B, or contain the equivalent information about the claim and the possibility of applying, and where and by when to apply to the Court. The form set out at Paragraph 2.1 is as follows:

> **"IN THE HIGH COURT OF JUSTICE**
> **[CHANCERY] [FAMILY] DIVISION**
>
> Case Number ……
>
> IN THE MATTER OF AN APPLICATION FOR A DECLARATION OF THE PRESUMED DEATH OF (INSERT NAME)
>
> A claim has been issued in the High Court of Justice, for a [declaration] [variation of a declaration] that (insert name), whose last known address was (insert address) is presumed to be dead. Any person having an interest may apply to the Court to intervene in the matter.
>
> If you wish to apply to the Court, you should do so at [Court address] as soon as possible, and if possible within 21 days of the date of this notice. Delay may harm your prospects of being able to intervene.

---

78 CPR r.57.21(1)(a)

79 CPR r.57.21(1)(b)

[If the claimant is legally represented]

(Name)

Claimant's Legal Representative

(Address)

[If the claimant is not legally represented]

(Claimant's address for service)"

The Court must refuse to hear an application where the notice and/or advertisement requirements have not been met.[80]

Seven days is not a lot of time to arrange publishing the claim, and if it is not possible to advertise seven days then the applicant should do so as soon as possible after that deadline has expired and seek relief pursuant to CPR r.3.1(2)(a) (see Subsection F(a) above) at the hearing of the application.

(g) Evidence

Sufficient interest

If an application is made by a person who is not one of those closely related family members set out at s.1(5)(a), the applicant will need to establish that they have sufficient interest in the seeking of a declaration of a presumed death in order for the Court to consider the application.

The applicant must therefore provide evidence focused on (i) why they consider that they have sufficient interest to make the application (see Section E above), (ii) the reason(s) why they are seeking the declaration,

80 PDA 2013, s.9(3)

and (iii) any other issues that the applicant requires the Court to determine.

Sufficient evidence

The application must be accompanied by sufficient evidence to satisfy the Court that a missing person has either (i) died, or (ii) not been known to be alive for at least seven years.

Chief Master Marsh explained in *Re AB (Presumed Death)* [2019] EWHC 2785 (Ch) at [9]:

> "It is clear the burden of proof under section 2(1) is on the balance of probabilities (see *Greathead* [21]). The cogency of the evidence that will be required under section 2(1)(a) (the missing person has died) is likely to be greater than under section 2(1)(b) (the person has not known to be alive for a period of at least 7 years). The test under the former is a positive one whereas under the latter is to establish the absence of knowledge of the person being alive."

The reader is referred to the following cases which provide an indication of the sort of evidence that has satisfied the Court a person has died (rather than not being known to be alive for at least seven years):

1. *Greathead v Greathead* [2017] EWHC 1154 (Ch);

2. *Halford v Halford* [2018] EWHC 3005 (Fam);

3. *EA v NA* [2018] EWHC 583 (Fam);

4. *Re Irish* [2020] EWHC 456 (Ch);

5. *Re AB (Presumed Death)* [2019] EWHC 2785 (Ch);

6. *Austin v Mitchell* [2020] EWHC 3486 (Ch);

7. *Re Thomas' Application* [2023] EWHC 1006 (Fam);

8. *Reynolds v Saul* [2024] EWHC 3593 (Ch).

Re P (Presumption of Death) [2021] EWHC 3099 (Fam) is an example of an application where there was not sufficient evidence of death, but the Court was satisfied that the person in question had been missing over seven years.

The above cases demonstrate (supported by the authors' own experience) that evidence concerning the following can be helpful/persuasive:

1. the events leading up to the missing person's disappearance and the circumstances in which the missing person was last seen or heard from;

2. steps taken to find the missing person (such as police reports, searches (such as dog searches, human searches, drone searches), advertisements, posters etc);

3. whether or not the missing person was suffering from any medical conditions;

4. details as to whether the missing person has suffered from, or was suffering from, mental health problems and details of their mood leading up to their disappearance;

5. details as to whether the missing person has any history of suicidal thoughts;

6. details as to the missing person's mood in the lead up to their disappearance;

7. whether there have been any financial transactions following the disappearance (current and savings account bank statements should be included);

8. whether the missing person went missing with any important personal effects such as passport, mobile phone, wallet, etc.;

9. whether the missing person had consumed any alcohol or taken any drugs before the disappearance;

10. whether there were any changes in the behaviour of the missing person in the period leading up to their disappearance;

11. details of any debt/poor economic circumstances;

12. details as to the terrain/environment in which the missing person disappeared; and

13. details as to the atmospheric/weather conditions on the day of the disappearance (strong winds, strong tides, heavy frosts or snow, excessive heat).

G. INTERVENERS

The only persons automatically entitled to intervene are (i) the missing person's spouse, civil partner, child or sibling (including half-blood siblings),[81] or (ii) the Attorney General (who may intervene in such proceedings, whether or not the Court directs papers relating to the application to be sent to the Attorney General).[82] Any other person may only intervene with the permission of the Court.[83]

Where the Attorney General incurs costs in connection with an application (for a declaration or variation order), the Court may make

81 PDA 2013, s.11(1)

82 PDA 2013, s.11(2)

83 PDA 2013, s.11(3)

such order as it considers appropriate as to the payment of costs by the parties to the proceedings.[84]

CPR r.57.22(a) provides that those automatically entitled to intervene must first notify the Court of the intention to intervene in accordance with the requirements of Practice Direction 57B.

Intervening in proceedings under s.11 includes:

1. arguing before the Court any question in relation to the application which the Court considers it necessary to have fully argued;[85]

2. in proceedings on an application for a declaration under the PDA 2013, seeking a determination or order under s.4;[86] and

3. in proceedings on an application for a variation order, seeking a determination or order under s.7.[87]

H. The First Hearing

(a) Background

A claim (whether for a declaration of presumed death or for a variation order) must be listed for a mandatory initial case management hearing ("**the First Hearing**") either:

---

[84] PDA 2013, s.10(3)-(4)

[85] PDA 2013, s.11(4)(a)

[86] PDA 2013, s.11(4)(b)

[87] PDA 2013, s.11(4)(c)

1. more than 28 days (but where practicable no more than 58 days) after issue;[88] or

2. where the claim form has been served outside the jurisdiction, more than seven days (but where practicable no more than 35 days) after the period for filing provided for by CPR r.57.19(7), to allow for time for those served with notice of the claim or who respond to the advertisement of the claim to file notice of intention to intervene or an application for permission to intervene as the case may be.[89]

The Court must notify all those who have filed notice of intention to intervene or an application for permission to intervene of the date of the directions hearing.[90]

The Chancery Guide at 23.37 explains:

> "A directions hearing will be invariably required; the role of the court in these proceedings is quasi-inquisitorial and the court must satisfy itself that the requirements of the Presumption of Death Act 2013 are fulfilled before making a declaration. It may for example (under section 12) at any stage require a non-party to provide information that it considers relevant to the question whether the missing person is alive or dead."

In *Re Irish*, HHJ Matthews (sitting as a Judge of the High Court) at [2] said:

> "The purpose of this directions hearing is at least twofold. First, it enables the court to check that all the requirements of the Act and the relevant CPR have been complied with.

88 Practice Direction 57B, Paragraph 1.4(a)

89 Practice Direction 57B, Paragraph 1.4(b)

90 Practice Direction 57B, Paragraph 1.5

> Second, if (whether as a result of the notifications of the proceedings or the advertisement in the press) any person does come forward wishing to intervene in the claim, the court can give directions as to filing and service of evidence, and any other relevant matters connected with the intervention."

(b) Preparation for the First Hearing

In the authors' experience, the First Hearing is usually listed for one hour. The claimant/applicant (or their solicitor) will be sent a notice of hearing which will set out the time, date, and length of the First Hearing. The notice of hearing will include directions in relation to practical issues such as filing bundles and skeleton arguments.

If there have been any developments since the application, or additional documentation has come to light that requires an explanation, then the claimant/applicant should consider preparing a second witness statement to deal with these points.

It is advisable to prepare a skeleton argument in advance of this hearing (usually drafted by counsel) to set out the position in respect of procedural compliance, evidence, and any other issues the claimant/applicant wishes the Court to consider (such as application for further information, or to accelerate the disposal hearing).

(c) Attending the First Hearing

The First Hearing will be heard by either a High Court Judge, a Master, a Circuit Judge entitled to sit in the High Court under s.9 of the SCA 1981, or a District Judge entitled to sit in the High Court under s.9 of the SCA 1981 in one of the district registries.

As the hearing is being heard in the High Court, only those with rights of audience (counsel or solicitors with higher rights of audience in civil

Courts) may advocate in Court, unless the applicant is acting on their own as a litigant in person.

At the First Hearing the judge will check compliance with the procedural rules and consider whether any further information is required. In appropriate cases the judge may consider treating the First Hearing as the final disposal hearing.

<u>Further information</u>

Pursuant to s.12(1) of the PDA 2013, the Court may by order at any stage require a person who is not a party to proceedings to provide it with specified information that it considers relevant to the question of whether the missing person is alive or dead. The Court may do so on the application of a party to the proceedings or of its own volition without an application being made.[91]

The First Hearing is a natural juncture for the Court to consider making such an order.

Any order made pursuant to s.12 may not require the provision of information:

1. which is permitted or required by any rule of law to be withheld on grounds of public interest immunity;[92]

2. which any person would be entitled to refuse to provide on grounds of legal professional privilege;[93] or

---

91 PDA 2013, s.12(3)

92 PDA 2013, s.12(4)(a)

93 PDA 2013, s.12(4)(b)

3. whose provision might incriminate the person providing it, or that person's spouse or civil partner, of an offence.[94]

Treating the First Hearing as a Disposal Hearing

Although the PDA 2013 anticipates an initial directions hearing followed by a final hearing, the Court can exercise its case management powers under CPR r.3.1.(2)(b) (power to bring forward a hearing) and (p) (take any other step or make any other order for the purpose of managing the case and furthering the overriding objective) to accelerate the final or disposal hearing of an application on the basis that all the formalities had been complied with, and that there is no one who having been given notice of the proceedings wishes to intervene or provide any further evidence.

The Court has accelerated applications under the PDA 2013 when it has considered it appropriate:

1. In *Re Irish* [2019] EWHC 2508 (Ch) the Court exercised its case management powers contained in CPR r.3.1(2)(b) and (m) (CPR r.3.1(2)(m) is now CPR r.3.1(2)(p)) to dispose of the case at the first hearing. HHJ Paul Matthews (sitting as a Judge of the High Court) at [7] emphasised, however, that it will not always be appropriate for the Court to take this course of action and that if "*statutory requirements are still to be fulfilled, directions given, or persons notified, the matter should proceed to a final hearing in the usual way.*"

2. In *Re AB (Presumed Death)* [2019] EWHC 2785 (Ch) Chief Master Marsh applied the procedure adopted in *Re Irish* to dispose of the case at the first hearing.

94 PDA 2013, s.12(4)(c)

3. In *Re Johnson* [2020] EWHC 207 (Ch), HHJ Paul Matthews (sitting as a Judge of the High Court) exercised the Court's case management powers under CPR r.3.1(2)(b) and (m) (now (p)) to accelerate the final or disposal hearing on the basis that all the formalities had been complied with, and that there was no one who having been given notice of the proceedings wished to intervene or provide any further evidence.

In addition to the cases set out above, the *Chancery Guide* at 23.38 explains "*[e]xceptionally, if all the papers are in order at the first directions hearing, the court may be prepared to treat the hearings as a final disposal hearing.*"

In the authors' experience, if an applicant considers that the application may be ready to be determined at the First Hearing, then they may wish to invite the Court to consider the following issues:

1. Have the procedural requirements/formalities set out in the PDA 2013, CPR rr.57.17-57.23, and CPR Practice Direction 57B, been complied with?

2. If the Court is satisfied that (i) the formalities have been complied with, (ii) that there is no one who having been given notice of the proceedings wishes to intervene or provide any further evidence, and (iii) the Court has sufficient evidence before it to consider the application, should the Court accelerate the final or disposal hearing to hear the application at the first hearing?

3. If the Court considers that there are any procedural requirements or formalities outstanding, or there is currently insufficient evidence to make a declaration, what directions should be made?

As to the matters which the Court must consider, should it be willing to dispose of the application at the First Hearing, please see Section I below.

Should the application not be disposed of at the First Hearing, then the application will be listed for a disposal hearing ("**the Disposal Hearing**").

I. The Disposal Hearing

(a) Preparing for the Disposal Hearing

If a Disposal Hearing is listed following the First Hearing, then this will usually be listed for one hour. As before, the applicant (or their solicitor) will be sent a notice of hearing which will set out the time, date, and length of the Disposal Hearing. The notice of hearing will include directions in relation to practical issues such as filing bundles and skeleton arguments.

If there have been any developments since the First Hearing, or additional documentation has come to light that requires an explanation, then the applicant should consider preparing a further witness statement to deal with these points.

A skeleton argument should be prepared in advance of the Disposal Hearing to set out the position in respect of procedural compliance, evidence, and the declaration/order sought.

(b) Attending the Disposal Hearing

The Disposal Hearing will usually be heard by the same judge who heard the First Hearing (which will have been heard by a High Court Judge, a Master, a Circuit Judge entitled to sit in the High Court under s.9 of the SCA 1981, or a District Judge entitled to sit in the High Court under s.9 of the SCA 1981 in one of the district registries).

At the Disposal Hearing, the claimant (or their advocate) must present the claim to the Court in the usual way and seek to convince the judge that:

1. the procedural formalities have been complied with; and

2. on considering the evidence, and on the balance of probabilities, the missing person has either died or has not known to be alive for a period of at least seven years.

As Chief Master Marsh explained in *Re AB (Presumed Death)* [2019] EWHC 2785 (Ch) at [9] (and as set out below), the test in respect of death is a positive one whereas in respect of the missing person not known to be alive for a period of at least seven years it is to establish the absence of knowledge of the person being alive.

Should the claimant satisfy the Court that the missing person is, on the balance of probabilities, to be presumed to be dead, or missing for a period of at least seven years, then the Court must make a declaration of presumed death pursuant to s.2(1) and consider the specific wording and form of the declaration.

J. The Declaration

(a) Form of declaration

Form CH42 is a useful template to consider in advance of, as well as at, the Disposal Hearing, as it sets out the matters that the declaration must cover.

<u>Date and time</u>

A problematic area can often be the question of the date and time of death that the Court must specify pursuant to s.2. The date and time of death is an important area to consider in advance of the Disposal Hearing as it can impact broader issues relating to the administration of the missing person's estate (e.g. pensions etc.).

Sections 2(3)-(4) provide:

> "(3) Where the court—

> (a) is satisfied that the missing person has died, but
>
> (b) is uncertain at which moment during a period the missing person died,
>
> the finding must be that the missing person is presumed to have died at the end of that period.
>
> (4) Where the court—
>
> (a) is satisfied that the missing person has not been known to be alive for a period of at least 7 years, but
>
> (b) is not satisfied that the missing person has died,
>
> the finding must be that the missing person is presumed to have died at the end of the period of 7 years beginning with the day after the day on which he or she was last known to be alive."

In *Greathead v Greathead* [2017] EWHC 1154 (Ch), HHJ Paul Matthews (sitting as a Judge of the High Court) was satisfied as to the date of disappearance (being the day that the missing person disappeared) but there was no evidence in respect of time of death. In that case, HHJ Paul Matthews recorded the time of death as midnight on the day of disappearance and justified his reasoning at 24 as being *"because it is the end of the period during which I consider on the evidence it is more likely than not that Edward died, namely, the day on which he disappeared."*

In *Re P (Presumption of Death)*, as there was no clear evidence regarding the circumstances of the missing person's disappearance, the Court was unable to make a declaration that that the missing person had died, so it instead made a declaration pursuant to s.2(4) that the missing person was presumed to have died at the end of the seven years beginning with the day on which he was last known to be alive.

In *Re Johnson,* HHJ Paul Matthews (sitting as a Judge of the High Court) was satisfied that the missing person was dead but was uncertain as to the moment of the missing person's death between the date of their disappearance and the date of the hearing. HHJ Paul Matthews said at [13]: *"I must include a finding that he is presumed to have died at the time of my decision that is at 11.30 AM on 5 February 2020. I do not regard this as according with common sense. But in my judgment it at least accords with what the law requires of me..."*

There may be factual elements to a case that may help the Court be as specific as it can as to the end of the relevant period. In one unreported case in which one of the authors appeared (*Re Houslip* (2024, Bristol District Registry)) the time of death was found to be nautical twilight in the specific area of the country in which the missing person disappeared on the date of their disappearance.

<u>Other matters</u>

In addition to making a declaration of presumed death, the Court also has discretionary powers to:

1. determine any question which relates to an interest in property and arises as a result of a variation order;[95]

2. determine the domicile of the missing person at the time of his or her presumed death;[96]

3. make such order as it considers reasonable in relation to any interest in property acquired as a result of a declaration;[97]

95 PDA 2013, s.4(1)(a) and s.7(a)

96 PDA 2013, s.(1)(b) and s.7(b)

97 PDA 2013, s.4(2)

4. direct that the value of any interest in property acquired as a result of the declaration is not to be recoverable by virtue of a variation order;[98]

5. direct that the value of any interest in property acquired as a result of the declaration is not to be recoverable (i) in any circumstances, or (ii) where conditions specified in the order are met;[99]

6. to vary or revoke a declaration;[100]

7. when making a variation order, to make such further order (if any) as it considers reasonable in relation to any interest in property acquired as a result of the declaration varied or revoked by the order;[101]

8. to direct the trustee of a trust affected by a declaration to take out an insurance policy in respect of any claim which may arise by virtue of an order to vary or revoke a declaration.[102]

(b) Effect of a declaration

Should a declaration of presumed death not be appealed and the period for appealing has passed (21 days from the date of the declaration), or an appeal has been unsuccessful,[103] then the declaration will be effective

---

98 PDA 2013, s.4(3)

99 PDA 2013, s.4(4)

100 PDA 2013, s.5(1)

101 PDA 2013, s.7(2)

102 PDA 2013, s.13(1)

103 PDA 2013, s.3(3)-(4)

against all persons[104] and conclusive of (i) the missing person's presumed death,[105] and (ii) the date and time of the presumed death.[106]

If the Court makes a declaration, then it must send a copy of the declaration to the Registrar General.[107] On receipt of a copy of a declaration, the Registrar General must:

> "(a) make an entry in the Register of Presumed Deaths containing the name of the missing person and such other information as may be prescribed in relation to that person's presumed death,
>
> (b) secure that the entry made in the Register of Presumed Deaths is included in the index of the registers of deaths, and
>
> (c) make traceable the connection between the entry in the Register of Presumed Deaths and the index of the registers of deaths."[108]

Similar provisions apply in relation to amendment and cancellation of entries in the Register of Presumed Deaths following a variation order (see Paragraph 2 of Schedule 1 to the PDA 2013).

---

104 PDA 2013, s.3(2)

105 PDA 2013, s.3(1)(a)

106 PDA 2013, s.3(1)(b)

107 PDA 2013, Schedule 1, Paragraph 1

108 PDA 2013, Schedule 1, Paragraph 1(2)

CHAPTER FIVE

ALTERNATIVES TO THE PDA 2013

A. IMPACT OF THE PDA 2013 ON OTHER LEGISLATION

The effect of s.16(1) of the PDA 2013 is that, since the enactment of the PDA 2013, it is no longer possible to apply under other legislation for a declaration of presumed death *if* that declaration can be made pursuant to s.1 of the PDA 2013.

Section 16(2) provides that, where a Court or tribunal makes a declaration of presumed death other than under the PDA 2013 (i.e. under any other legislation), ss.2(2)-(4) apply to the Court or tribunal as they apply to the High Court when making a declaration under the PDA 2013, and the Court or tribunal must therefore specify the time and date of death using the prescribed formula set out at s.2.

Subject to those matters set out above, and the amendments and repeals set out at Schedule 2 to the PDA 2013, s.16(4) provides that all other legislation applies as it did before the enactment of the PDA 2013.

B. PRESUMPTION OF DEATH ORDERS UNDER S.37 OF THE CPA 2004

(a) Background

Section 37(1)(c) of the CPA 2004 provides that either the High Court or the Family Court may, in accordance with Chapter 2 of Part 2 of the CPA 2004 "*make an order (a 'presumption of death order') which dissolves a civil partnership on the ground that one of the civil partners is presumed to be dead.*" However, as a consequence of s.16(1) of the PDA 2013, the High Court or Family Court can only consider an application under s.37(1)(c) of the CPA 2004 where the High Court does not have jurisdiction to make a declaration of presumed death under the PDA 2013. An example of where there might not be jurisdiction under the PDA 2013 is where a civil partnership was registered in England and Wales but the parties to the civil partnership have since moved abroad.

Section 55 of the CPA 2004 sets out the requirements in respect of an application under s.37(1) (c) of the CPA 2004 and provides that:

> "(1) The court may, on an application made by a civil partner, make a presumption of death order if it is satisfied that reasonable grounds exist for supposing that the other civil partner is dead.
>
> (2) In any proceedings under this section the fact that—
>
>> (a) for a period of 7 years or more the other civil partner has been continually absent from the applicant, and
>>
>> (b) the applicant has no reason to believe that the other civil partner has been living within that time,
>
> is evidence that the other civil partner is dead until the contrary is proved."

Section 222 of the CPA 2004 is clear that the Court only has jurisdiction to entertain proceedings for a presumption of death order on an application by a civil partner pursuant to s.37(1)(c), if:

1. at the time the application is made, the High Court does not have jurisdiction to entertain an application by that civil partner under s.1 of the PDA 2013 for a declaration that the other civil partner is presumed to be dead; and

2. the two people concerned registered as civil partners of each other in England and Wales and it appears to the Court to be in the interests of justice to assume jurisdiction in the case.

(b) **Petition**

Pursuant to FPR PD 5A paragraphs 1.1 and 1.2 and Table 1, applications should be made using Form D8D. The form itself is self-explanatory and contains detailed guidance/prompts. The details that would be contained in a witness statement accompanying a PDA 2013 Claim Form are contained within Form D8D[109]. The authors recommend reading the Supplementary Notes to Form D8D prior to completing Form D8D.[110]

A certified copy of the civil partnership certificate must be filed with the Court alongside the completed Form. This should be accompanied by any documents regarding a change of name. It is crucial the certificates/documents are certified – the Court will not accept photocopies.

If the civil partnership certificate is in a foreign language, a translation of the certificate into English, or Welsh in a Court in Wales, from an authorised person for translations must be provided. The translation should be signed by a notary public or authenticated by a statement of truth.

A supplementary witness statement may be required, either alongside the Form or filed subsequently, if (i) the boxes within the Form are too small to contain all the relevant information, (ii) there are any unusual features

---

109 Form D8D is available at <https://assets.publishing.service.gov.uk/media/5aa6aef4ed915d4f563b7032/d8d-eng.pdf> accessed on 14 October 2025

110 The Supplementary Notes are available at <https://assets.publishing.service.gov.uk/media/5aa6af2a40f0b66b5fb4b579/d8d-notes-eng.pdf> accessed 14 October 2025

of the case, and/or (iii) after the application is made, any new information comes to light or issue arises which requires explanation or could be relevant to the determination of the application.

C. Leave to swear to death orders

(a) Background

Where a grant is sought in respect of the estate of a missing person, and it is not possible to pursue proceedings pursuant to the PDA 2013, the person who would be entitled to a grant faces a problem as they will be unable to swear to the death of the missing person due to the lack of evidence (e.g. no death certificate). In such cases, r.53 of the N-CPR 1987 provides that:

> "An application for leave to swear or give evidence as to the death of a person in whose estate a grant is sought may be made to a district judge or registrar, and shall be supported by an affidavit or a witness statement setting out the grounds of the application and containing particulars of any policies of insurance effected on the life of the presumed deceased together with such further evidence as the district judge or registrar may require."

The Court has power pursuant to r.53 of the N-CPR 1987 to give the person next entitled to the grant the leave to swear to the death of a missing person on either a particular date, or at some point since.

Williams, Mortimer & Sunnucks at 17-30 explains that the principal circumstances in which applications for leave to swear death are made are where the presumed deceased has:

> "(i) not been heard of for a considerable period by those with whom they might be expected to communicate; or

> (ii) disappeared in circumstances pointing to suicide or accidental death."

Consequently, any time after a person has gone missing, an applicant may apply for an order of leave to swear to death. Should an order of leave to swear to death be made then an application for probate can be made in respect of the missing person. However, unlike a declaration of presumed death pursuant to the PDA 2013, an order of leave to swear death is not conclusive of the missing person's death.

Williams, Mortimer & Sunnucks at 17-30 explains:

> "It is not the practice to make orders for leave to swear death save on the most convincing evidence. Even then, the court does not actually presume the missing person to be dead and should that person prove to be alive, they may apply to a district judge or registrar or higher judge (depending on who made the order) for its rescission of the order and for revocation of the grant."

(b) Procedure

The application for leave to swear death should be made to a district judge or registrar.[111] The application is made *ex parte* and must be supported by a witness statement or affidavit setting out all the relevant matters upon which the applicant relies.

Williams, Mortimer & Sunnucks suggest at 17-34 that the affidavit or witness statement should:

- set out the grounds of the application and depose to the applicant's belief that the presumed deceased is dead;

---

111 N-CPR 1987, r.53

- give the age of the presumed deceased;
- describe the circumstances in which the presumed deceased was last heard of;
- provide copies or details of any relevant communications from the presumed deceased;
- provide details of searches and inquiries conducted and advertisements placed seeking information on their whereabouts with copies of any relevant documents;
- provide copies of any reports received from the emergency services;
- exhibit a copy of any will left by the presumed deceased;
- if there is no will, give details of any next of kin;
- give particulars of any bank accounts or credit cards including the dates when they were last operated; and give particulars of any policies of assurance on the life of the presumed deceased.

D. COMMON LAW PRESUMPTION OF DEATH

Sachs J in *Chard v Chard* [1955] 3 All ER 721 explains the operation of the "common law presumption of death" at 728E-729A as follows:

> "… in matters where no statute lays down an applicable rule, the issue whether a person is, or is not, to be presumed dead is, generally speaking, one of fact and not subject to a presumption of law. To that there is an exception which can be assumed without affecting the present case. By virtue of a long sequence of judicial statements, which either assert or assume such a rule, it appears accepted that there is a

> convenient presumption of law applicable to certain cases of seven years' absence where no statute applies. That presumption in its modern shape takes effect (without examining its terms too exactly) substantially as follows. Where … there is no acceptable affirmative evidence that [a missing person] was alive at some time during a continuous period of seven years or more, then if it can be proved first, that there are persons who would be likely to have heard of him over that period, secondly, that those persons have not heard of him, and thirdly, that all due inquiries have been made appropriate to the circumstances, [the missing person] will be presumed to have died at some time within that period. (Such a presumption would, of course, be one of law and could not be one of fact, because there can hardly be a logical inference from any particular set of facts that a man had not died within two thousand five hundred and fifty-five days but had died in two thousand five hundred and sixty.)"

Following the enactment of the PDA 2013, the common law presumption of death will be of little use to practitioners, although it is briefly mentioned here as it could, theoretically, be an option in exceptional circumstances.

CHAPTER SIX

GUARDIANSHIP ORDERS

A. BACKGROUND

Although the PDA 2013 provides a relatively simple procedure to apply for a declaration of presumed death, it does not assist in dealing with the property and financial affairs of a missing person whilst that person is considered missing. The G(MP)A 2017 was introduced to address this situation, and it empowers the Court to appoint a guardian who can act on behalf of a missing person and administer their property and financial affairs (referred to as a "guardianship order").[112] In addition to the appointment of a guardian, the G(MP)A 2017 provides the Court with a wide range of powers including to provide directions and make declarations concerning guardians, and to vary and revoke guardianship orders. Therefore, as with the PDA 2013, guardianship orders are very much focused on Type 1 Cases.

The G(MP)A 2017 is supplemented by the *Guardianship (Missing Persons) Act 2017 – Code of Practice* ("**the Code of Practice**"), which provides statutory guidance for guardians appointed under the G(MP)A 2017, and persons making applications under the G(MP)A 2017. Pursuant to s.22(2) of the G(MP)A 2017 a guardian must have regard to the Code of Practice. The authors strongly recommend that any prospective claimant or applicant reads the Code of Practice prior to issuing a claim.

This chapter is predominantly concerned with how to prepare an application for a guardianship order, but reference is also made (although

112 G(MP)A 2017, s.2(1)

not in detail) to other applications that may be made under the G(MP)A 2017.

B. WHEN IS A PERSON DEEMED MISSING?

In the context of the G(MP)A 2017, a "missing person" is someone who is absent from (i) his or her usual place of residence,[113] or (ii) his or her usual day-to-day activities,[114] and either of the following conditions are met:

1. If the person's whereabouts are not known at all,[115] or are not known with sufficient precision to enable the person to be contacted for the purposes of decisions relating to his or her property and financial affairs;[116] or

2. The person is unable to make decisions relating to his or her property and financial affairs or to communicate such decisions with a view to their implementation (or both),[117] and the reason for that is something beyond the person's control, other than illness, injury or lack of capacity in relation to a matter (within the meaning of the MCA 2005).[118]

A person who is detained, whether in a prison or another place, is to be treated for the purposes of the G(MP)A 2017 as absent from his or her usual place of residence and usual day-to-day activities.[119]

---

113 G(MP)A 2017, s1(1)(a)

114 G(MP)A 2017, s1(1)(b)

115 G(MP)A 2017, s.1(2)(a)

116 G(MP)A 2017, s.1(2)(b)

117 G(MP)A 2017, s.1(3)(a)

118 G(MP)A 2017, s.1(3)(b)

119 G(MP)A 2017, s.1(4)

C. JURISDICTION

Section 2(2)-(3) of the G(MP)A 2017 sets out the Court's jurisdiction in respect of applications under the G(MP)A 2017 and provides that the Court has jurisdiction to hear and determine an application under the G(MP)A 2017 in relation to property or financial affairs of a missing person only if:

1. the person was domiciled in England and Wales on the day before he or she was first known to be missing;

2. the person had been habitually resident in England and Wales throughout the period of one year ending with that day; or

3. the application is made by the person's spouse or civil partner and the applicant;

    a. is domiciled in England and Wales on the day on which the application is made, or

    b. has been habitually resident in England and Wales throughout the period of one year ending with that day.

If a person is missing for two or more separate periods, the reference above to "*the person was domiciled in England and Wales on the day before he or she was first known to be missing*" is to be read as a reference to the day before the latest period began.[120]

[120] G(MP)A 2017, s.2(3)

D. CIRCUMSTANCES WHEN THE COURT MAY MAKE AN ORDER

If the Court has jurisdiction to hear an application under the G(MP)A 2017 then it may make a guardianship order if the Court is satisfied that either of the following conditions is met:[121]

1. the "absence condition", which is where:

    a. the person whose property or financial affairs are the subject of the application is missing;[122]

    b. the person was missing throughout the period of 90 days ending with the day on which the application was made;[123]

    c. in all the circumstances, the appointment of a guardian in respect of property or financial affairs of the missing person is in the missing person's best interests (which is dealt with at s.18); [124] and

    d. there is a person who could be appointed as guardian (see the requirements at s.4(1));[125] or

2. the "urgency condition", which is where:

    a. the absence condition does not apply because (and only because) the absence condition is not met;[126] but

---

121 G(MP)A 2017, s.3(1)

122 G(MP)A 2017, s.3(2)(a)

123 G(MP)A 2017, s.3(2)(b)

124 G(MP)A 2017, s.3(2)(c)

125 G(MP)A 2017, s.3(2)(d)

126 G(MP)A 2017, s.3(3)(a)

b. a decision is needed, or is likely to be needed, in relation to property or financial affairs of the missing person before the day on which that condition would be met.[127]

E. POWERS

The G(MP)A 2017 provides the Court with powers to:

1. determine the domicile of a missing person at the time an application for a guardianship order is being considered;[128]

2. make a guardianship order;[129]

3. give directions to a guardian about whether/how to act in a particular case, or the scope of their authority under the guardianship order and the G(MP)A 2017;[130]

4. make a declaration on action taken by a guardian which is outside the scope of a guardian's authority;[131]

5. make a declaration as to whether a guardian performed or failed to perform a duty under a guardianship order;[132]

6. if the court makes a declaration as to a guardian's performance pursuant to s.11, it may make an order disallowing expenses incurred by a guardian or remuneration to which a guardian

---

127 G(MP)A 2017, s.3(3)(b)

128 G(MP)A 2017, s.2

129 G(MP)A 2017, s.3

130 G(MP)A 2017, s.10

131 G(MP)A 2017, s.11(1)(a)

132 G(MP)A 2017, s.11(1)(b)

would be entitled, or requiring a guardian to make a payment to the missing person or their estate;[133]

7. vary a guardianship order;[134] and

8. revoke a guardianship order.[135]

F. CLAIMANTS

Although s.2 of the G(MP)A 2017 states "*[a] person may apply to the court for an order appointing a guardian in respect of some or all of a missing person's property and financial affairs (a 'guardianship order')*", this is caveated by s.19(1) which provides that the Court must refuse to hear an application for a guardianship order (or any other application pursuant to ss.9-13) if the claimant does not have a sufficient interest in relation to the missing person's property or financial affairs.

Section 19(3) provides that the following persons are to be automatically treated as having sufficient interest:

1. the missing person;[136]

2. the missing person's personal representatives;[137]

3. the missing person's spouse;[138]

---

133 G(MA)A 2017, s.11(3)

134 G(MP)A 2017, s.12(1)

135 G(MP)A 2017, s.13(1)

136 G(MP)A 2017, s.19(3)(a)

137 G(MP)A 2017, s.19(3)(a)

138 G(MP)A 2017, s.19(3)(b)

4. the missing person's civil partner;[139]

5. the missing person's parent;[140]

6. the missing person's child;[141]

7. the missing person's sibling (this includes siblings of full and half-blood); [142]

8. in relation to applications for a guardianship order only, a person who was the guardian in respect of some or all of the missing person's property and financial affairs at any time during the period of one year ending with the day on which the application is made; [143]

9. in relation to an application for directions by the court to guardians, variation, or revocation, the guardian.[144]

The list of persons set out at s.19(3) is a non-exhaustive one and applicants may be found to have sufficient interest in many other circumstances. Paragraphs 4.21 to 4.28 of the *Code of Practice* provide further guidance on what is meant by sufficient interest and provides the following persons who may have sufficient interest in certain circumstances: a long-term cohabiting partner; a business partner; a step-parent; a step-sibling; a step-child; and a close friend.

139 G(MP)A 2017, s.19(3)(b)

140 G(MP)A 2017, s.19(3)(b)

141 G(MP)A 2017, s.19(3)(b)

142 G(MP)A 2017, s.19(3)(b)

143 G(MP)A 2017, s.19(3)(c)

144 G(MP)A 2017, s.19(3)(d)

G. MAKING AN APPLICATION

(a) Rules, procedure, and venue

The procedure for applying for a guardianship order is set out in the G(MP)A 2017, Section VI of CPR Part 57 (rr.57.25-57.33), and Practice Direction 57C.

All proceedings under the G(MP)A 2017 must be issued in the High Court in either the Chancery Division or the Family Division.[145]

The CPR applies to proceedings under the G(MP)A 2017 which are issued in the Family Division, except that the provisions of the FPR relating to the drawing up and service of orders apply instead of the provisions in Part 40 of the CPR and Practice Direction 40B.[146]

(b) Claim Form

A claim for a guardianship order (or any other order under the G(MP)A 2017) must be made in accordance with CPR Part 28 as modified by CPR r.57.28, and by issuing a Claim Form in accordance with CPR Part 8.[147]

The Claim Form must:

1. be in Form N208;[148]

---

145 CPR r.57.26(1)

146 CPR r.57.26(2)

147 CPR r.57.27(1)

148 Form N208 is available at <https://www.gov.uk/government/publications/form-n208-claim-form-cpr-part-8> accessed on 14 October 2025

2. state that Part 8 of the CPR applies;[149]

3. contain a brief outline of the facts;

4. state the question which the applicant/claimant wants the Court to decide;

5. the remedy sought and the legal basis for the claim to that remedy (i.e. the granting of a guardianship order);[150]

6. that the claim is made under the G(MP)A 2017;[151]

7. if the claimant is claiming in a representative capacity, what that capacity is;[152]

8. if the defendant is sued in a representative capacity, what that capacity is;[153]

9. include the following information set out at Paragraph 1.1 of Practice Direction 57C:

    a. information about the claimant:

        i. the claimant's name and address (and, if different, their address for service);[154]

---

149 CPR r.8.2(a)

150 CPR r.8.2(b)(ii)

151 CPR r.8.2(c)

152 CPR r.8.2(d)

153 CPR r.8.2(e)

154 Practice Direction 57C, paragraph 1.1(1)(a)

ii. the relationship of the claimant to the missing person;[155]

iii. if the claimant is not the missing person's spouse, civil partner, parent, child or sibling, or other person within s.19(3) of the G(MP)A 2017, details of the claimant's interest in relation to the missing person's property and financial affairs;[156] and

b. the name and last known address of the missing person (who must be named as defendant), and when and for how long they have been missing;[157]

c. details of the terms of the guardianship order sought including the name of the proposed guardian;[158]

d. if applicable, that the claimant seeks a guardianship order on the basis that the urgency condition applies (see above and s.3.3 of the G(MP)A 2017);[159] and

10. be accompanied by a witness statement attaching any relevant evidence and providing the following information required by Paragraph 1.2 of Practice Direction 57C:

f. as far as the claimant knows:

---

155 Practice Direction 57C, paragraph 1.1(1)(b)

156 Practice Direction 57C, paragraph 1.1(1)(c)

157 PD 57C, para 1.1(2)

158 PD 57C, para 1.1(3)

159 PD 57C, para 1.1(4)(c)

i. the missing person's name and surname, and any other names by which the missing person is or have formerly been known;[160]

ii. the missing person's gender;[161]

iii. the missing person's maiden surname (if any);[162]

iv. the missing person's date and place of birth;[163]

v. the occupation of the missing person;[164]

vi. the existence, name and surname, and the current residential or electronic address and any nominated address for service of:

    1. the missing person's spouse or civil partner;[165]

    2. the missing person's parents;[166]

    3. the missing person's siblings;[167]

---

160 PD 57C, para 1.2(1)(a)

161 PD 57C, para 1.2(1)(b)

162 PD 57C, para 1.2(1)(c)

163 PD 57C, para 1.2(1)(d)

164 PD 57C, para 1.2(1)(e)

165 PD 57C, para 1.2(1)(f)(i)

166 PD 57C, para 1.2(1)(f)(ii)

167 PD 57C, para 1.2(1)(f)(iii)

4. the missing person's children;[168]

vii. the missing person's National Insurance number;[169]

viii. the missing person's usual place of residence, and when they became absent from it;[170]

ix. the missing person's usual day-to-day activities and when they became absent from them;[171]

x. whether it is asserted that the missing person is in prison or has been detained, and if so where and from what date;[172]

xi. the date and circumstances in which the missing person is thought to have become missing; and whether there has been any police investigation, and, if so, whether any such report has been or could be obtained;[173]

xii. the missing person's whereabouts, and any evidence or contentions with regard to the matters set out in s.1(2) of the G(MPA) 2017 (the missing person's whereabouts – first condition);[174]

---

168 PD 57C, para 1.2(1)(f)(iv)

169 PD 57C, para 1.2(1)(g)

170 PD 57C, para 1.2(1)(h)

171 PD 57C, para 1.2(1)(i)

172 PD 57C, para 1.2(1)(j)

173 PD 57C, para 1.2(1)(k)

174 PD 57C, para 1.2(1)(l)

xiii. any evidence or contentions with regard to the matters set out in s.1(3) of the G(MP)A 2017 (the missing person's ability to make relevant decisions – the second condition);[175]

xiv. reasons for supposing that the missing person is still alive;[176] and

xv. what, if any, steps are proposed with regard to service of the claim upon or other notification of the claim to be given to the missing person, with reasons for such steps being considered appropriate;[177]

g. reasons why the claimant considers the court has jurisdiction to hear and determine the claim under s.2(2) (applying for a guardianship order) of the G(MP)A 2017;[178]

h. reasons why the claimant asserts that they satisfy the requirement to have a sufficient interest in relation to the missing person's property or financial affairs, having regard to section 19 (requirement for applicants to have sufficient interest) of the G(MP)A 2017;[179]

---

175 PD 57C, para 1.2(1)(m)

176 PD 57C, para 1.2(1)(n)

177 PD 57C, para 1.2(1)(o)

178 PD 57C, para 1.2(2)

179 PD 57C, para 1.2(3)

i. if not the claimant, the name and address of the proposed guardian together with evidence that the person consents to acting as guardian;[180]

j. details of the missing person's property and financial affairs as are known to the claimant and relevant to the claim for a guardianship order;[181]

k. reasons why, in all the circumstances, the appointment of a guardian in respect of property or financial affairs of the missing person is in the missing person's best interests (ss.3(2)(c) and 18 of the G(MP)A 2017); [182]

l. an explanation as to why the proposed guardian meets the requirements to act as guardian set out in section 4 (choice of guardian) of the G(MP)A 2017;[183]

m. details of any persons referred to in CPR r.57.29(1)(a) to whom the claimant cannot send notice of the claim and reasons for this;[184]

n. details of the public news media in which the claimant proposes to advertise the claim (CPR r.57.29(1)(b)) and reasons why it is appropriate;[185]

o. details of any registered Lasting Power of Attorney or registered Enduring Power of Attorney, or confirmation

---

180 PD 57C, para 1.2(4)

181 PD 57C, para 1.2(5)

182 PD 57C, para 1.2(6)

183 PD 57C, para 1.2(7)

184 PD 57C, para 1.2(8)

185 PD 57C, para 1.2(9)

that no Lasting Power of Attorney or Enduring Power of Attorney has been registered, by or in relation to the missing person;[186] and

p. details of any Deputy appointed or confirmation that no Deputy has been appointed on behalf of the missing person under the MCA 2005;[187]

10. where the absence condition is not or may not be met, the witness statement must provide reasons why the claimant considers the urgency condition (s.3(3) of the 2017 Act) is met, and attach any evidence which supports this;[188]

11. if the court is to serve the claim form, be accompanied by one copy of the claim form for each respondent.[189]

The witness statement that must accompany the Claim Form should provide sufficient detail as to why the applicant considers they have sufficient interest, particularly if they are not one of the persons who are automatically deemed to have sufficient interest pursuant to the G(MP)A 2017. The witness statement must be verified by a statement of truth.[190]

Compliance with Practice Direction 57C should be checked prior to issuing a claim/application as non-compliance can result in delays in a claim/application being heard, and can risk the claim/application being struck out.

---

186 PD 57C, para 1.2(10)

187 Practice Direction 57C, paragraph 1.2(11)

188 Practice Direction 57C, paragraph 1.3

189 CPR r.6.4(3)

190 Practice Direction 22, paragraph 2.1

(c) Issue Fee

The issue fee will be:

- £646 if filed in the Chancery Division;[191] or
- £279 if filed in the Family Division.

(d) Service/notice

Pursuant to s.20(1)(a) of the G(MP)A 2017, the claimant must send notice of an application under the G(MP)A 2017 to the persons specified at CPR r.57.29(1)(a).

CPR r.57.29(1)(a) provides that a claimant or applicant must, within 14 days of notification of the date of the first hearing of the claim for a guardianship order or of an application for a revocation/variation order, send notice of the claim or application, along with the material set out in Paragraph 3.1. of Practice Direction 57C (subject to any redaction ordered by the court, and subject to if the person has a nominated address for service known to the claimant or applicant, and provided that such address for service has been nominated expressly for the purpose of G(MP)A 2017 proceedings, the material need only be sent to that address; and, if the claimant or applicant has no access to any, or no, e-mail address of their own, they need not send the material to any e-mail address),[192] to the following persons whose identity and current residential or e-mail address or nominated address for service are known to the claimant or applicant:[193]

---

191 CPFO 2008, Schedule 1 , fee 1.5

192 CPR r.57.29(2)

193 CPR r.57.29(1)(a)

1. the spouse or civil partner of the missing person;[194]

2. any parent of the missing person;[195]

3. any child of the missing person;[196]

4. any sibling of the missing person;[197]

5. if there are no persons as set out above, the nearest relative of the missing person known to the claimant or applicant;[198]

6. any guardian or any former guardian of the missing person;[199]

7. any person who has previously intervened in and/or become a party to these or any proceedings in which a guardianship order was sought in relation to the missing person.[200]

Paragraph 3.1. of Practice Direction 57C provides that the material required to be sent as notice by r.57.29 (or r.57.30) must include (subject to any redactions ordered by the court):

1. a copy of the claim form or application notice;

2. a copy of the evidence in support; and

[194] CPR r.57.29(1)(a)(i)

[195] CPR r.57.29(1)(a)(ii)

[196] CPR r.57.29(1)(a)(iii)

[197] CPR r.57.29(1)(a)(iv)

[198] CPR r.57.29(1)(a)(v)

[199] CPR r.57.29(1)(a)(vi)

[200] CPR r.57.29(1)(a)(vii)

3. a letter stating the date of the first hearing of the claim or application and including the following wording:

> "Any spouse, civil partner, parent, child or sibling of the missing person is entitled to intervene in the matter. Any other person having an interest may apply to the court for permission to intervene in the matter.
>
> If you wish to give notice of intention to intervene or to apply to the court for permission to intervene, you should do so at [COURT ADDRESS] as soon as possible, and no later than 14 days before the date of the first hearing, and serve a copy of that notice or application on the [CLAIMANT/APPLICANT] at the address given below. Delay may harm your prospects of obtaining permission to intervene if you are not entitled to intervene, and in any event, may be taken into account on any question relating to costs."

If an application is made relating to a guardianship order or the potential exercise of powers under the G(MP)A 2017, then the applicant must give notice and advertisement pursuant to CPR r.57.30.

(e) Advertisement

Pursuant to s.20(1)(b) of the G(MP)A 2017, a claimant or applicant must also advertise the claim in accordance with CPR r.57.29(1)(b) and Paragraph 4.1 of Practice Direction 57C.

The claimant or applicant must, within 14 days of notification of the date of the first hearing of the claim for a guardianship order or of an application for a revocation/variation order, advertise notice of the claim or application:

1. in a form which meets the requirements set out in Paragraph 4.1 of Practice Direction 57C;[201] and

2. in at least one public news media circulating in or relating to the vicinity of the last known usual place of residence of the missing person; being "Advertisement of the claim/application." [202]

Paragraph 4.1 of Practice Direction 57C provides that the advertisement of the claim for a guardianship order or an application for a revocation/variation order required by s.20(1) (giving notice of applications) of the G(MP)A 2017 and CPR r.57.29(1)(b) must be in the appropriate form set out below, or contain the equivalent information about the claim or application and the possibility of applying, and where and by when to apply, to the court:

"IN THE HIGH COURT OF JUSTICE

IN THE [CHANCERY] [FAMILY] DIVISION

Case Number ......

IN THE MATTER OF AN APPLICATION MADE UNDER THE GUARDIANSHIP (MISSING PERSONS) ACT 2017 [FOR A GUARDIANSHIP ORDER] [TO REVOKE OR VARY A GUARDIANSHIP ORDER] IN RESPECT OF [INSERT MISSING PERSON NAME]

[A claim has been issued in the High Court of Justice, [ ] Division, Claim No. [ ], by [INSERT NAME OF CLAIMANT] for an order that [INSERT NAME OF PROPOSED GUARDIAN] be appointed guardian in respect of [INSERT NAME OF MISSING PERSON ("the

---

[201] CPR r.57.29(1)(b)(i)

[202] CPR r.57.29(1)(b)(ii)

missing person")], whose [last usual place of residence] was [INSERT ADDRESS].]

[An application has been issued in the High Court of Justice, [ ] Division, Claim No. [ ], by [INSERT NAME OF APPLICANT] for an order that the Guardianship Order dated [ ] made in respect of [INSERT NAME OF MISSING PERSON ("the missing person")], whose [last usual place of residence] was [INSERT ADDRESS] should be [revoked] [varied].]

The date and venue for the first hearing of the [Claim] [Application] is [ ] at [address].

Any spouse, civil partner, parent, child or sibling of the missing person is entitled to intervene in the matter. Any other person having an interest may apply to the Court for permission to intervene in the matter.

If you wish to give notice of intention to intervene or to apply to the Court for permission to intervene, you should do so at [COURT ADDRESS] as soon as possible, and no later than 14 days before the date of the first hearing, and serve a copy of that notice or application on the [CLAIMANT/APPLICANT] at the address given below. Delay may harm your prospects of obtaining permission to intervene if you are not entitled to intervene, and, in any event, may be taken into account on any question relating to costs.

Claimant/Applicant's name

[If the claimant/applicant is legally represented]

Name of Claimant/Applicant's Legal Representative and their address for service

[If the claimant/applicant is not legally represented]

Claimant/Applicant's address for service"

(f) Written Statement confirming procedural compliance

Once a claimant or applicant has served and advertised in accordance with CPR r. 57.29(1), the claimant or applicant must file at court no later than seven days before the first hearing of the claim or application, a witness statement[203] confirming procedural compliance including:

1. compliance with CPR r.57.29(1)(a), and attaching Form N215 (Certificate of Service) completed to describe each method of sending to each person, as if references on that form to "service" were to "sending";[204] and

2. compliance with CPR r.57.29(1)(b), and containing or attaching evidence of Advertisement of the claim/application, including details of how, where and when it was advertised.[205]

The witness statement must be verified by a statement of truth.[206]

H. INTERVENERS

If a claim or application is made under the G(MP)A 2017, there is an opportunity for certain persons to intervene in those proceedings.

---

203 CPR r.57.29(3)

204 CPR r.57.29(3)(a)

205 CPR r.57.29(3)(b)

206 Practice Direction 22, paragraph 2.1

(a) Automatic right to intervene

A spouse, civil partner, child or sibling has an automatic right to intervene in respect of any application made under the G(MP)A 2017.[207] CPR r.57.31(1) and Paragraph 5.1 of Practice Direction 57C provides that notice by those automatically entitled to intervene should be given by an intervener filing with the court, and serving on the claimant, not less than 14 days before the first hearing date of the claim or application, written notice that specifies the intervener's:

1. name and address;[208]

2. relationship to the missing person; [209]

3. reasons for intervening;[210] and

4. particulars of any determination, order or directions sought.[211]

Failure to comply with the requirements of CPR r.57.31(1) set out above shall not prevent a person from intervening (if they are otherwise entitled to do so) but it may be taken into account on any question relating to costs.[212]

---

207 G(MP)A 2017, s.21(1)

208 Practice Direction 57C, paragraph 5.1(1)

209 Practice Direction 57C, paragraph 5.1(2)

210 Practice Direction 57C, paragraph 5.1(3)

211 Practice Direction 57C, paragraph 5.1(4)

212 CPR r.57.31(3)

(b) No automatic right to intervene

Individuals who do not have an automatic right to intervene may only intervene with the court's permission[213] if they can demonstrate that they have sufficient interest in the property and financial affairs of the missing person.[214] Pursuant to CPR r.57.31(3), such an applicant who does not have an automatic right to intervene must, not less that 14 days before the first hearing, file an application for permission to intervene in accordance with CPR Part 23 and Paragraph 5.2 of Practice Direction 57C, and serve the application on the claimant.

Pursuant to CPR Part 23 and Paragraph 5.2 of Practice Direction 57C, the application to intervene must specify:

1. the applicant's name and address;[215]

2. why the applicant asserts that they satisfy the requirement to have a sufficient interest in relation to the missing person's property or financial affairs, having regard to ss.19 and 21(3) of the G(MP)A 2017 (the requirement for applicants to have sufficient interest);[216]

3. the applicant's relationship to the missing person or other interest in the proceedings; [217]

4. the reasons for applying for permission to intervene; [218] and

---

213 G(MP)A 2017, s.21(2)

214 G(MP)A 2017, s.21(3)

215 Practice Direction 57C, paragraph 5.2(1)

216 Practice Direction 57C, paragraph 5.2(2)

217 Practice Direction 57C, paragraph 5.2(3)

218 Practice Direction 57C, paragraph 5.2(4)

5. particulars of any determination, order or directions sought.[219]

CPR r.57.31(5) provides that within seven days of receiving an application for permission to intervene:

1. from a person who has not been sent or served with the claim form or the application notice, the claimant/applicant must serve a copy of the claim form or application, the evidence in support and notice of the hearing date, upon the person seeking permission to intervene;[220] and in any case

2. the claimant or applicant must file with the court and serve upon the person seeking permission to intervene, a statement of whether or not they object and any evidence in support of any objection.[221]

Where the Court grants permission to intervene to a person who does not have an automatic right to intervene, it may do so on conditions and may give case management directions.[222] The Court may also direct that a person who intervenes in proceedings be added as a claimant (provided that they consent in writing) or defendant to the claim.[223]

---

219 Practice Direction 57C, paragraph 5.2(5)

220 CPR r.57.31(5)(a)

221 CPR r.57.31(5)(b)

222 CPR r.57.31(6)

223 CPR r.57.31(7)

I. DEATH OF THE MISSING PERSON POST-ISSUE AND PRIOR TO A HEARING

If a missing person has died before or dies after the issue of the claim then, subject to any order of the Court, the claim shall not abate or be stayed, and CPR r.19.12 shall not apply.[224]

Should a prospective claimant consider that there is real doubt as to whether the missing person is still alive, then the prospective claimant can draft the Claim Form to incorporate claims under both the PDA 2013 and the G(MP)A 2017.[225] If the Court then determines during those proceedings that the missing person has not been known to be alive for a period of seven years then the Court can order that the claim continue as if it had been brought under the PDA 2013.[226]

J. THE FIRST HEARING

(a) Background

A first hearing of the claim shall be listed by the Court not less than 56 days from the date of issue (but any person may apply for the court for the claim (or an application) to be heard at an earlier date) ("**the First Hearing**").[227]

The *Chancery Guide* at 23.43 explains:

> "The court will fix a directions/disposal hearing when the claim is issued to establish that: (1) the claim and the evidence provide the information that is required by the 2017 Act and the CPR; and (2) that the claim has been

[224] CPR r.57.33(1)

[225] CPR r.57.33(2)

[226] CPR r.57.33(3)

[227] CPR r.57.27(2)

> notified and advertised. Any applications to intervene will also be dealt with at the directions hearing. In a straightforward case, the court may be able to make an order appointing a guardian at the first hearing."

The *Chancery Guide* continues at 23.44:

> "If there is a dispute about the appointment, or further steps are required, directions will be given, and a disposal hearing date will be fixed. It is very unlikely the court will permit a trial of disputed issues of fact other than in exceptional circumstances."

(b) Preparation for the First Hearing

The First Hearing will usually be listed for one hour. The claimant/applicant (or their solicitor) will be sent a notice of hearing which will set out the time, date, and length of the First Hearing. The notice of hearing will include directions in relation to practical issues such as filing bundles and skeleton arguments.

If there have been any developments since the application, or additional documentation has come to light that requires an explanation, then then claimant/applicant should consider preparing a second witness statement to deal with these points.

It is advisable to prepare a skeleton argument in advance of the First Hearing (usually drafted by counsel) to set out the position in respect of jurisdiction, procedural compliance, evidence, and any other issues the claimant/applicant might need to address (applications to intervene, etc.)

(c) Attending the First Hearing

The First Hearing will be heard by either a High Court Judge, a Master, a Circuit Judge entitled to sit in the High Court under s.9 of the SCA

1981, or a District Judge entitled to sit in the High Court under s.9 of the SCA 1981 in one of the district registries.

As the hearing is being heard in the High Court, only those with rights of audience (counsel or solicitors with higher rights of audience in civil courts) may advocate in court, unless the claimant/applicant is acting on their own as a litigant in person.

At the First Hearing the judge will check compliance with the procedural rules and consider whether the claim can be disposed of at the First Hearing. If the claim appears straightforward then the Court may be able to make an order appointing a guardian at the First Hearing (as to what matters the Court will need to consider, please see Section K below). If the Court is not satisfied that it can dispose of the claim at the First Hearing, then directions will be given and a hearing date will be fixed for a disposal hearing.

K. MATTERS TO CONSIDER AT A DISPOSAL HEARING

If the Court is happy to dispose of the claim at the First Hearing, or if a further disposal hearing is listed, the Court will need to consider the matters set out below. A skeleton argument should be prepared which addresses all of these issues.

(a) Conditions

As set out above at Section D, if the Court has jurisdiction to hear an application under the G(MP)A 2017 then it may make a guardianship order if the Court is satisfied that the "absence condition" has been met or, if the absence condition does not apply because (and only because) the absence condition is not met, then the "urgency condition" is met. Submissions should be made in respect of the conditions in line with Section D above.

(b) Appointment of a guardian

If the Court is satisfied that it can make a guardianship order, then the Court must consider the appointment of a guardian.

<u>Who can be a guardian?</u>

A guardian may only be appointed if the Court is satisfied that the prospective guardian:

1. is an individual aged at least 18 or a trust corporation (as defined in s.68 of TA 1925);[228]

2. consents to the appointment; [229]

3. is suitable to act as the guardian of the property or financial affairs; [230] and

4. if appointed, will act in the missing person's best interests.[231]

In determining for the purposes of G(MP)A 2017 what is in a missing person's best interests, the Court or a guardian:

1. must consider all the relevant circumstances of which the court or guardian is aware;[232] and

228 G(MP)A 2017, s.4(1)(a)

229 G(MP)A 2017, s.4(1)(b)

230 G(MP)A 2017, s.4(1)(c)

231 G(MP)A 2017, s.4(1)(d)

232 G(MP)A 2017, s.18(1)(a)

2. must, among other things, take the steps described in ss.18(2)-(4).[233]

Section 18(2) provides that the Court or guardian must consider, so far as is reasonably ascertainable:

1. any relevant wishes and feelings expressed by the missing person at any time, including any relevant written statement made by the missing person;

2. the beliefs and values that would be likely to influence the missing person; and

3. any other factors that the missing person would be likely to consider.

Section 18(3) states that the Court or guardian must take into account the views of any persons of whom the Court or guardian (as appropriate) is aware with a relevant interest in relation to the missing person's property or financial affairs, where it is reasonably practicable and appropriate to do so.

Section 18(4) provides that the Court or guardian must consider the consequences of taking a proposed action.

Nothing in the G(MP)A 2017 requires the Court or a guardian:

1. to decide a matter by reference to the decision the missing person is likely to have taken in relation to the matter,[234] or

---

[233] G(MP)A 2017, s.18(1)(b)

[234] G(MP)A 2017, s.18(5)(a)

2. to consider any question as to whether or when the missing person might cease to be missing. [235]

Who is suitable?

For the purposes of determining whether a person (defined in as "the proposed guardian"[236]) is suitable to act as the guardian of property or financial affairs, the Court must, among other things, have regard to:

1. the proposed guardian's relationship with the missing person;[237]

2. the missing person's views on the proposed guardian, so far as they are known to, or reasonably ascertainable by, the Court;[238]

3. whether the proposed guardian has the skills and knowledge necessary to carry out the functions proposed to be conferred on the proposed guardian by the guardianship order;[239]

4. any conflict between the proposed guardian's interests and the missing person's interests.[240]

Conflicts of interest

For the purposes of determining whether there is a conflict between the proposed guardian's interests and the missing person's interests, the Court must, among other things, consider:

---

[235] G(MP)A 2017, s.18(5)(b)

[236] G(MP)A 2017, s.4(2)

[237] G(MP)A 2017, s.4(2)(a)

[238] G(MP)A 2017, s.4(2)(b)

[239] G(MP)A 2017, s.4(2)(c)

[240] G(MP)A 2017, s.4(2)(d)

1. any connection between the proposed guardian's property and financial affairs and the missing person's property and financial affairs;[241] and

2. how any such connection might affect the taking of decisions by the proposed guardian if appointed.[242]

There will not be a conflict between the proposed guardian's interests and the missing person's interests merely because the proposed guardian:

1. is the missing person's spouse, civil partner, parent, child, sibling or other relative;[243]

2. was living with the missing person immediately before that person became a missing person;[244] or

3. may benefit from being appointed as guardian, whether directly or indirectly.[245]

Appointment

The Court may:

1. make a guardianship order appointing a person as a guardian whether or not the person is proposed in the application for the order;[246]

---

241 G(MP)A 2017, s.4(3)(a)

242 G(MP)A 2017, s.4(3)(b)

243 G(MP)A 2017, s.4(4)(a)

244 G(MP)A 2017, s.4(4)(b)

245 G(MP)A 2017, s.4(4)(c)

246 G(MP)A 2017, s.4(5)

2. appoint two or more guardians in respect of some or all of a missing person's property and financial affairs;[247]

3. appoint two or more guardians at the same time or also at different times;[248]

4. appoint two or more guardians by means of the same guardianship order or separate guardianship orders;[249]

5. appoint two or more guardians whether or not the appointment of two or more guardians is proposed in an application for, or for the variation of, a guardianship order.[250]

The Schedule to the G(MP)A 2017 makes further provision concerning the appointment of two or more guardians and provides that:

> "**1 Powers of court when appointing two or more guardians**
>
> (1) This paragraph applies where, when making or varying a guardianship order, the court appoints two or more guardians in respect of some or all of a missing person's property and financial affairs, whether by appointing them at the same time or at different times.
>
> (2) The court must—
>
> > (a) provide for the guardians to act jointly in relation to the property or financial affairs,

[247] G(MP)A 2017, s.16(1)

[248] G(MP)A 2017, s.16(2)(a)

[249] G(MP)A 2017, s.16(2)(b)

[250] G(MP)A 2017, s.16(3)

(b) provide for each guardian to have sole responsibility in relation to different parts of the missing person's property and financial affairs, or

(c) provide for a combination of joint and sole responsibilities.

(3) For the purposes of sub-paragraph (2)(c), the court provides for a combination of joint and sole responsibilities if it provides—

(a) for the guardians to act jointly in relation to parts of the missing person's property and financial affairs, and

(b) for one or more of the guardians to have sole responsibility in relation to other parts of the missing person's property and financial affairs.

(4) The court may make different provision in relation to different guardians so far as it provides for them to have sole responsibility in relation to different parts of the missing person's property and financial affairs, including provision imposing different conditions and restrictions.

(5) The court may provide that different guardians are appointed for different periods.

2 Power of court to remove guardians

(1) This paragraph applies where a guardianship order appoints two or more guardians.

(2) The court's powers under section 12 to vary the order include a power to remove one or more of the guardians without appointing a replacement (but not to remove all of the guardians without replacing any of them).

3 Guardians appointed to act jointly

(1) This paragraph applies where a guardianship order appoints two or more guardians to act jointly in relation to property or financial affairs.

(2) The guardians must act unanimously in relation to the property or financial affairs.

(3) A condition or restriction imposed by the court in respect of the property or financial affairs applies to each of the guardians.

(4) A direction given by the court under section 10 in respect of the property or financial affairs applies to each of the guardians.

4 Death of a guardian

(1) This paragraph applies where—

(a) a guardianship order appoints two or more guardians, and

(b) one of the guardians dies.

(2) The order is not revoked under section 14(1)(c) on the guardian's death unless—

(a) no other guardian appointed under the order remains alive, or

(b) the only other guardian remaining alive is appointed only to act jointly with the deceased guardian.

(3) If, by virtue of this paragraph, the order is not revoked on the guardian's death, a guardian appointed under the order who remains alive must apply to the court for the variation or revocation of the order as soon as reasonably practicable after becoming aware of the death.

5 Expiry of period of appointment of a guardian

(1) This paragraph applies where—

(a) a guardianship order appoints two or more guardians, and

(b) a guardian's period of appointment expires.

(2) The order is not revoked under section 14(1)(d) if the period of appointment of another guardian appointed under the order has not expired.

(3) But section 15(2) applies in relation to a person who deals with the guardian mentioned in sub-paragraph (1)(b) after that guardian's period of appointment expires as if the guardianship order had been revoked under section 14(1)(d) on the expiry of that period."

(c) Duration and expiry

A guardian is appointed for the period specified in the guardianship order.[251]

---

251 G(MP)A 2017, s.7(1)

The Court can impose a maximum duration of four years beginning with the day on which the order is made.[252]

L. SENDING GUARDIANSHIP ORDERS TO THE PUBLIC GUARDIAN

Pursuant to s.3(4) of the G(MP)A 2017 and CPR r.57.32, the Court must send a copy of any guardianship order it makes to the Public Guardian.

M. RIGHTS AND POWERS OF GUARDIANS

(a) Powers and rights

A guardianship order must appoint the guardian to exercise on behalf of the missing person:

1. all of the missing person's rights and powers in relation to the property or financial affairs to which the order relates;[253] or

2. such of those rights and powers as are specified or described in the order.[254]

A guardianship order may (i) impose duties on the guardian,[255] and (ii) include conditions and restrictions.[256]

The Court's powers when making a guardianship order include powers:

---

[252] G(MP)A 2017, s.7(2)

[253] G(MP)A 2017, s.6(1)(a)

[254] G(MP)A 2017, s.6(1)(b)

[255] G(MP)A 2017, s.6(2)(a)

[256] G(MP)A 2017, s.6(2)(b)

1. to require the guardian to give the Public Guardian security for the exercise of the guardian's functions;[257]

2. to require the guardian to submit to the Public Guardian such reports at such times or intervals as the court may direct;[258]

3. to make provision suspending the guardian's authority to exercise rights and powers for a period.[259]

The rights and powers that a guardian may be appointed to exercise include:

1. selling, letting or mortgaging the missing person's property;[260]

2. making investments;[261]

3. executing deeds and other documents;[262]

4. recovering money owed to the missing persons;[263]

5. discharging debts and other obligations of the missing person (whether legally enforceable or not);[264]

---

[257] G(MP)A 2017, s.6(3)(a)

[258] G(MP)A 2017, s.6(3)(b)

[259] G(MP)A 2017, s.6(3)(c)

[260] G(MP)A 2017, s.6(4)(a)

[261] G(MP)A 2017, s.6(4)(b)

[262] G(MP)A 2017, s.6(4)(c)

[263] G(MP)A 2017, s.6(4)(d)

[264] G(MP)A 2017, s.6(4)(e)

6. resigning trusteeships held by the missing person;[265]

7. bringing or conducting legal proceedings;[266] and

8. making a gift out of the missing person's property.[267]

A guardian may only make a gift out of the missing person's property if the guardianship order expressly authorises the making of the gift, the making of gifts of a description which includes the gift or the making of gifts generally.[268]

A guardian may not (i) execute a will for the missing person,[269] or (ii) exercise a power vested in the missing person as a trustee in relation to another person's property.[270]

(b) Expenses and remuneration

A guardian is entitled to be reimbursed out of the missing person's property for reasonable expenses incurred in connection with the exercise of functions as a guardian[271] and the Court may direct that a guardian is entitled to remuneration payable out of the missing person's property for exercising functions as a guardian.[272]

---

265 G(MP)A 2017, s.6(4)(f)

266 G(MP)A 2017, s.6(4)(g)

267 G(MP)A 2017, s.6(4)(h)

268 G(MP)A 2017, s.6(7)

269 G(MP)A 2017, s.6(6)(a)

270 G(MP)A 2017, s.6(6)(b)

271 G(MP)A 2017, s.9(1)

272 G(MP)A 2017, s.9(2)

A guardian must:

1. keep records of the exercise of functions as a guardian, including accounts relating to the exercise of those functions;[273] and

2. on ceasing to be a guardian, give a copy of the records to such persons as the Court directs.[274]

The Court may, on an application, order a person to provide the applicant with accounts or other information relating to the person's exercise of functions as a guardian in the form and manner specified in the order. [275]

When a Court is (i) directing a guardian to give a copy of their records to such persons as the Court directs, or (ii) considering an application to order a person to provide the applicant with accounts or other information relating to the person's exercise of functions as a guardian in the form and manner specified in the order, the Court must have regard to:

1. the need to keep the missing person's affairs confidential;[276] and

2. the need to impose only such requirements as are reasonable in all the circumstances (and, regarding applications, see also ss.19 and 20).[277]

---

[273] G(MP)A 2017, s.9(3)(a)

[274] G(MP)A 2017, s.9(3)(b)

[275] G(MP)A 2017, s.9(4)

[276] G(MP)A 2017, s.9(5)(a)

[277] G(MP)A 2017, s.9(5)(b)

(c) Restrictions

When directing a guardian to give a copy of their records to such persons as the Court directs, or ordering a person to provide the applicant with accounts or other information relating to the person's exercise of functions as a guardian in the form and manner specified in the order, such orders may include conditions and restrictions.[278]

N. DIRECTIONS TO GUARDIANS

The Court may give a direction to a guardian about: (i) whether or how to act in a particular case;[279] or (ii) the scope of the guardian's authority under the guardianship order and the G(MP)A 2017.[280] The Court may do so on an application or without an application being made (and see ss.19 and 20).[281]

O. DECLARATIONS CONCERNING GUARDIAN'S AUTHORITY

The Court may make a declaration:

1. that action taken by a guardian, when purporting to exercise functions as a guardian, was within or outside the scope of the guardian's authority under the guardianship order and the G(MP)A 2017;[282] or

2. that a guardian performed or failed to perform a duty under the guardianship order, the G(MP)A 2017 or regulations under s.58

[278] G(MP)A 2017, s.9(6)

[279] G(MP)A 2017, s.10(1)(a)

[280] G(MP)A 2017, s.10(1)(b)

[281] G(MP)A 2017, s.10(2)

[282] G(MP)A 2017, s.11(1)(a)

of the MCA 2005 or a duty owed to the missing person under a rule of law. [283]

The Court may do so on an application or without an application being made (and see ss.19 and 20).[284]

If the Court makes a declaration as set out above (i.e. s.11(1)) that a guardian acted outside the scope of the guardian's authority or failed to perform a duty as described in that subsection, it may:

1. make an order disallowing expenses incurred by the guardian or remuneration to which the guardian would otherwise be entitled;[285]

2. make an order requiring the guardian to make a payment of an amount determined by the court to the missing person or the missing person's estate;[286]

3. make such other order as the court considers appropriate for the purpose of compensating the missing person or the missing person's estate for any loss resulting from the action or failure.[287]

The above (i.e. s.11(3)) does not prevent the Court from exercising powers available to it otherwise than by virtue of that subsection.[288]

If the Court makes a declaration under s.11(1), or otherwise determines, that a guardian acted outside the scope of the guardian's authority or

283 G(MP)A 2017, s.11(1)(b)

284 G(MP)A 2017, s.11(2)

285 G(MP)A 2017, s.11(3)(a)

286 G(MP)A 2017, s.11(3)(b)

287 G(MP)A 2017, s.11(3)(c)

288 G(MP)A 2017, s.11(4)

failed to perform a duty as described in that subsection but (i) the guardian shows that the guardian behaved honestly and reasonably in doing so,[289] and (ii) the Court considers that, having regard to all the circumstances, the guardian ought to be relieved of personal liability,[290] the Court may relieve the guardian, either entirely or partly, of personal liability in respect of the action or failure.

In considering whether to relieve a guardian of personal liability, the Court must have regard to (i) the care and skill that it is reasonable to expect the guardian to have exercised in the circumstances,[291] and (ii) in the case of a person acting as a guardian in the course of a business or profession, any special knowledge or experience that it is reasonable to expect of a person acting in the course of that kind of business or profession.[292]

P. VARIATION

The Court may make an order varying a guardianship order, on an application or without an application being made.[293] It may do so only if it is satisfied that:

1. the person whose property or financial affairs are the subject of the guardianship order is missing;[294]

2. the absence condition or the urgency condition is met;[295] and

---

[289] G(MP)A 2017, s.11(5)(a)

[290] G(MP)A 2017, s.11(5)(b)

[291] G(MP)A 2017, s.11(6)(a)

[292] G(MP)A 2017, s.11(5)(b)

[293] G(MP)A 2017, s.12(1)

[294] G(MP)A 2017, s.12(2)(a)

[295] G(MP)A 2017, s.12(2)(b)

3. in all the circumstances, the proposed variation is in the missing person's best interests (see s.18 (and ss.19-20)).[296]

The power to vary a guardianship order includes power to:

1. appoint a different person to be the guardian;[297]

2. add or remove property or financial affairs, subject to s.12(4);[298]

3. add, remove or alter conditions or restrictions;[299]

4. alter the period for which the guardian is appointed, subject to s.12(5);[300]

5. do anything else that the Court could do on making a guardianship order.[301]

Where the Court varies a guardianship order in circumstances in which the urgency condition (but not the absence condition) is met, it may only make provision in respect of property or financial affairs in respect of which it is satisfied that the urgency condition is met.[302]

---

296 G(MP)A 2017, s.12(2)(c)

297 G(MP)A 2017, s.12(3)(a)

298 G(MP)A 2017, s.12(3)(b)

299 G(MP)A 2017, s.12(3)(c)

300 G(MP)A 2017, s.12(3)(d)

301 G(MP)A 2017, s.12(3)(e)

302 v G(MP)A 2017, s.12(4)

The Court may not vary a guardianship order so that the period for which the guardian is appointed ends after the last day of the four year period specified in s.7(2).[303]

The Court must send a copy of an order varying a guardianship order to the Public Guardian.[304]

Q. REVOCATION

The Court may make an order revoking a guardianship order, on an application or without an application being made.[305] If a guardian has reasonable grounds to believe that the person whose property or financial affairs are the subject of the guardianship order is no longer missing, the guardian must apply to the Court as soon as reasonably practicable for the revocation of the order.[306]

The Court may revoke a guardianship order only if it is satisfied that:

1. the person whose property or financial affairs are the subject of the guardianship order is no longer missing;[307] or

2. in all the circumstances, revocation is in the missing person's best interests (see ss.18-20)).[308]

---

303 G(MP)A 2017, s.12(5)

304 G(MP)A 2017, s.12(6)

305 G(MP)A 2017, s.13(1)

306 G(MP)A 2017, s.13(2)

307 G(MP)A 2017, s.13(3)(a)

308 G(MP)A 2017, s.13(3)(b)

The Court must send a copy of an order revoking a guardianship order to the Public Guardian.[309]

(a) Automatic revocation

A guardianship order is automatically revoked:

1. on the death of the missing person;[310]

2. on the making of a declaration of presumed death in respect of the missing person under s.2 of the PDA 2013;[311]

3. on the death of the guardian;[312]

4. on the expiry of the guardian's period of appointment.[313]

A guardianship order made after the death of the missing person is to be treated as having been immediately revoked.[314]

Where a person becomes aware that a guardianship order appointing the person as guardian has been revoked (i) on the death of the missing person, or (ii) on the making of a declaration of presumed death under s.2 of the PDA 2013, the person must inform the Public Guardian as soon as reasonably practicable.[315]

---

309 G(MP)A 2017, s.13(4)

310 G(MP)A 2017, s.14(1)(a)

311 G(MP)A 2017, s.14(1)(b)

312 G(MP)A 2017, s.14(1)(c)

313 G(MP)A 2017, s.14(1)(b)

314 G(MP)A 2017, s.14(2)

315 G(MP)A 2017, s.14(3)

(b) Revocation by application

An application for a revocation or variation of a guardianship order must be made in accordance with Part 23 of the CPR 1998 and paragraph 2 of Practice Direction 57C.

(c) Protection following variation or revocation

Where a guardian acts within the scope of the authority conferred by the guardianship order and the G(MP)A 2017 at a time when (i) the guardianship order has been revoked, but (ii) the guardian does not know that, the guardian does not incur any personal liability (either to the missing person or any other person) because of the revocation.[316]

Where a person deals with a guardian at a time when (i) the guardianship order has been varied or revoked, but (ii) the person does not know that, the transaction between them is, in favour of that person, as valid as if the guardianship order had not been varied or revoked.[317]

Where the interest of a purchaser depends on whether a transaction between a guardian and another person was valid (as set out above), it is to be conclusively presumed in favour of the purchaser that the other person did not at the material time know of the variation or revocation of the guardianship order if:

1. the transaction between the guardian and the other person was completed within the period of 12 months beginning with the day on which the guardianship order was made;[318] or

2. before the completion of the purchase, or within the period of three months beginning with the day of its completion, the other

---

[316] G(MP)A 2017, s.15(1)

[317] G(MP)A 2017, s.15(2)

[318] G(MP)A 2017, s.15(3)(a)

person makes a statutory declaration that the person did not at the material time know of the variation or revocation of the guardianship order.[319]

For the purposes of s.15 of the G(MP)A 2017:

1. knowledge that a guardianship order has been revoked includes knowledge of the occurrence of an event which caused it to be revoked under s.14;[320] and

2. "purchaser" and "purchase" have the meaning given in s.205(1) of the Law of Property Act 1925.[321]

R. SECURITY BONDS

Where the Court makes a guardianship order which requires the guardian to give security for the discharge of his functions as guardian, the guardian must give the security before discharging any functions under the guardianship order, unless the Court permits the security to be given subsequently.[322]

Paragraph 10.2 of Practice Direction 57C provides that paragraphs 10.3 to 10.5 of Practice Direction 57C apply where the security is required to be given before the guardian discharges any functions under the guardianship order. Paragraphs 10.3 to 10.5 of Practice Direction 57C state:

> "10.3 Subject to paragraph 10.4, the security must be given in accordance with the requirements of regulation 33(2)(a) of the Lasting Powers of Attorney, Enduring Powers of

---

[319] G(MP)A 2017, s.15(1)

[320] G(MP)A 2017, s.15(4)(a)

[321] G(MP)A 2017, s.15(4)(b)

[322] Practice Direction 57C, paragraph 10.1

Attorney and Public Guardian Regulations 2007 (which makes provision about the giving of security by means of a bond that is endorsed by an authorised insurance company or an authorised deposit-taker).

10.4 The court may impose other requirements in relation to the giving of the security as it considers appropriate (whether in addition to, or instead of, those specified in paragraph 10.3).

10.5 In specifying the date from which the guardianship order referred to in paragraph 10.1 is to take effect, the court will consider the need to postpone that date for such reasonable period as would enable the Public Guardian to be satisfied that—

(1) if paragraph 10.3 applies, the requirements of regulation 34 of the Lasting Powers of Attorney, Enduring Powers of Attorney and Public Guardian Regulations 2007 have been met in relation to the security; and

(2) any other requirements imposed by the court under paragraph 10.4 have been met."

CHAPTER SEVEN

RE BENJAMIN ORDERS

A. Background

On 1 September 1892, Philip Benjamin stepped onto a train in Aix-la-Chapelle bound for London. He was never seen or heard from again.

Search enquiries and advertisements in every English colony and elsewhere in the world turned up nothing. His father, David Benjamin, had made a will in 1891 which left his residuary estate on trust, to be divided into as many shares as he had children at the date of his death. Just 28 days after Philip's fateful embarkment, David Benjamin executed a codicil which altered Philip's share in the event he survived his father. Following the death of David Benjamin, the trustees – nearly a decade on from David Benjamin's death – sought a determination from the Court as to how Philip's share should be distributed.

In *Re Benjamin* [1902] 1 Ch. 723, Joyce J in a short judgment held that the onus fell on the administrators to prove Philip was to be presumed dead, and once the presumption is raised, the onus fell on those claiming under Philip to show that he survived his father. Joyce J determined there was no doubt that Philip should be presumed to have predeceased David Benjamin in light of the high probability Philip died on 1 September 1892 or shortly thereafter.

Joyce J held the administrators were at liberty to divide Philip's share on the footing that Philip was unmarried and did not survive David Benjamin. It is important to note the distinction between the *Re Benjamin* jurisdiction and the PDA 2013 jurisdiction: Philip was specifically not declared dead. Joyce J stressed the existence and preserved the right of Philip or his representatives to make a claim to his share if evidence was subsequently forthcoming that he survived David

Benjamin. It will thus be clear that Benjamin Orders are designed solely for Type 2 Cases, although in many cases the missing person's family will also need to apply for declarations of presumed death or guardianship orders to deal with and administer their estate.

In the decades following *Re Benjamin*, orders following the principles laid down in that case – "Benjamin Orders" as they became known – were an important tool for the probate practitioner dealing with Type 2 Cases.

There was a spike in use following World War II. Many such cases involved airmen or soldiers missing in action who did not re-surface after World War II ended. Following this spike, however, Benjamin Orders largely fell out of (reported) use as technological advances and globalism meant fewer people went missing without trace.

The remit of Benjamin Orders in the probate and estates context appeared to diminish even further following the enactment of the PDA 2013 and G(MP)A 2017. Recent judgments have confirmed the crucial and wider role for Benjamin Orders. However, the Benjamin Order, in this context, is to cases concerning to a missing beneficiary of a trust or estate and the distribution of their share under a will, intestacy or trust settlement.

B. Remit

A Benjamin Order is appropriate where the evidence of death or life is less than conclusive. This is in contrast to the PDA 2013 where the evidence must be relatively concrete or has a seven year wait if the person is not known to be dead.

A Benjamin Order approves a proposal by personal representatives to distribute the estate and trust assets on a certain footing. Approval is often sought in respect of bequests and shares the missing person stands to inherit, but can also be sought to establish the interest of another (e.g. where A receives a bequest if their non-beneficiary parents, who include the missing person, pre-deceased the Deceased). Usually, but not always, personal representatives will seek approval to distribute an estate on the premises the missing person predeceased the Deceased. Benjamin Orders can also be deployed to enable distribution on the basis the missing person died in certain circumstances, such as without issue.

Benjamin Orders therefore serve a dual purpose. First, the approval of the Court to distribute on the footing the missing person is deceased. Second, to distribute on the footing of the missing person's circumstances at an ascribed point of death.

Practitioners should take care to consider the second purpose, rather than just deem it part-and-parcel of the first. Specific provision may be needed if the relevant will provides for the missing person's share to be passed to their issue or estate should they pre-decease the Deceased. If the will does not contain a clause covering the possibility of a beneficiary having predeceased the Deceased, personal representatives may need to seek an order permitting distribution on the footing the missing person died without issue or having married.

It may also be necessary to include provision that the missing person died without having triggered conditions placed on their share under the will. For example, a bequest may be conditional on the missing person not being not being married or still practising a given religion. If the will does place more unusual conditions on the missing person's share, specific consideration should be given to whether the conditions were or were not triggered before the missing person disappeared and if the condition is void.

The only necessary provision if the Deceased died intestate is the missing person was without issue. Under the intestacy rules,[323] an intestacy beneficiary's share does not pass to their spouse/civil partner or their estate, but does pass to their issue.

---

[323] AEA 1925, s.46

C. DO YOU NEED A BENJAMIN ORDER?

Benjamin Orders are appropriate where there is doubt as to whether any person is alive and that person would be prejudiced by the proposed distribution.

It is difficult to conceive that a Benjamin Order will be appropriate in the case of missing testators. However, a Benjamin Order may be required alongside a PDA 2013 declaration when the missing person's circumstances on death require prescription.

As the missing person must be prejudiced by the proposed distribution, Benjamin Orders are unlikely to be needed in the following circumstances:

- If the missing person's inheritance is conditional on an event which did not occur. For example, if the missing person inherits only if another surviving beneficiary pre-deceased the testator.

- If there has been ademption of the missing person's gift. Although, a Benjamin Order will be required if there is only partial ademption.

- The estate is insolvent and falls to be administered under the provisions of the Administration of Insolvent Estates of Deceased Persons Order 1986.

- A will under which the missing person inherits is found to be invalid for whatever reason and they are not a beneficiary under a previous will or intestacy.

- A Benjamin Order may also be unnecessary where the missing person is an absolute discretionary beneficiary. The personal representatives are at liberty to not distribute to the missing person in any event. Personal representatives may wish to seek the Court's blessing for the exercise of their discretion; see Lewin from [39-085] and *Public Trustee v Cooper* [2001] W.T.L.R. 901 for a detailed discussion.

D. LEGAL PRINCIPLES

What follows is a summary of the applicable principles. Practitioners must remember that equity – for that is where the *Re Benjamin* principles exist – will be flexible. At first glance, many cases may not fit neatly within the principles, particularly those from older authorities. Practitioners should not be deterred from pursuing an application in atypical or unusual cases, and should consider whether a sufficient analogy can be drawn with the existing principles and/or whether the circumstances could attract a departure from the more restrictive authorities.

The authorities arising from World War II sought to explain the circumstances in which a Benjamin Order will be granted in the following ways:

- Benjamin Orders "*are made, not as of course, but only on satisfactory prima facie evidence of practical impossibility of proof of the fact or event sought to be established*" – *Re Gess* [1942] Ch. 37 at 39.

- The Court should, "*without making any positive order declaring rights, protect personal representatives or trustees by giving them liberty to distribute on a particular footing based on probable inference*" – *Hansell v Spink* [1943] Ch. 396 at 399.

- "*It would... be open to the judge, if satisfied that every reasonable step had been taken in an attempt to trace individuals entitled to the fund, and that it was most improbable that any individual would ever establish [a claim]*" – *Re Lowe's Will Trusts* [1973] 1 W.L.R. 882 at 887.

Those authorities make clear the central consideration is the (im)probability of the missing person's death and traceability.

The relevant principles were cleared up and stated with greater clarity by Nourse J, as he then was, in *Re Green's Will Trusts* [1985] 3 All E.R. 455. His Lordship outlined the touchstone for determination where there is a possibility of the beneficiaries resurfacing, which will usually be the case, at 462:

> "I do not think that the question whether such an order should be made depends on whether or not there will be administrative inconveniences caused by the trustees retaining the fund. I think it depends on whether in all the circumstances the trustees ought to be allowed to distribute and the beneficiaries to enjoy their apparent interests now rather than later."

Nourse J's judgment has been cited numerous times since and provides an additional touchstone to the central consideration. Practitioners should nonetheless draw upon each of the authorities, particularly if strict application of the above passage would create difficulties due to administrative inconvenience being the primary motivating factor for personal representatives.

David Richards J, as he then was, added a further consideration in *Re MF Global UK Ltd (in special administration) (No 3)* [2013] 1 WLR 3874 at [32]: "*The purpose of the court's inherent jurisdiction is to enable practical effect to be given to a trust.*"

Whilst this passage is not directly on-point in the estates context – *Re MF* relates to administration of investment banks – David Richards J's judgment could be relied upon if the need for a Benjamin Order is driven by the practical realities of the estate and its administration. In any event, the authors take the view that such practical issues necessarily fall into Nourse J's reference to "*all the circumstances*".

Drawing these authorities together, the applicable principles can be summarised as follows:

- The central consideration is whether the missing person is dead, can be traced or will reappear on the probable inference(s) from the facts of the case, but need not be premised on other circumstances being an impossibility.

- The Court must be satisfied all reasonable steps have been taken to trace the missing person.

- Is it just for the beneficiaries to enjoy their interests now rather than at some unknown later date.

- Practicality should be considered in light of the nature and purpose of the trust.

E. Application of the Principles

The steps to be taken and the ascertainment of the probable inferences is set out below in Section G. What is reasonable will inherently depend on the nature and size of the estate, the missing person's share and the circumstances of the case.

(a) The Probable Inferences

Unsurprisingly, the last known circumstances of the missing person and the potential ways in which they may/may not have died will be of central importance:

- There are certain situations in which death is a near inevitable conclusion. *Re Fisher* is such an example: a suicide note followed by a person never being seen again is points persuasively to death. Likewise, if someone failed to resurface from a SCUBA dive, the overwhelming inference is death.

- Conversely, as will be seen below in *Re Vanstone*, where the missing person is known to have been street homeless but simply cannot be traced, the inference of death is looser.

- Another difficult situation is where the missing person moved to a lesser developed or war-stricken country, in which there is an inherent difficulty of tracing them.

The individual characteristics and circumstances of the missing person will also play a significant role:

- Age: An older missing person may be more likely to have predeceased the Deceased than a younger person.

- Health: Consider whether the missing person has chronic illnesses, health conditions which impinge on their life, health conditions, disabilities. Also consider addiction issues; alcoholism and drug issues may lead to a greater probability the missing person has died.

- Lifestyle: Linked to the above, lifestyle factors can include and range from homelessness to extreme sports.

Ultimately, this question will vary significantly from case to case. In some cases, it will be clear cut, such as a situation akin to that in *Re Fisher*. In others, the argument for a Benjamin Order will need to draw more from the below principles.

(b) Enjoyment Now or Later

The individual circumstances of the beneficiaries, the missing person and the personal representatives will need to be investigated and set out in the application/witness evidence. The following non-exhaustive factors are relevant:

- The age of the beneficiaries: This can be framed in a number of different ways. If the beneficiaries are in the later stages of their lives, it can be said that any delay would result in their potential share never being enjoyed. If younger, a lump sum of money could have a greater impact than if received later in life, however, they are in a position to wait longer for their share to (potentially) be realised.

- Impact on life: The financial and personal circumstances of the beneficiaries and the missing person will be relevant. Practitioners should consider whether the proposed distribution is impacted by the beneficiaries' particular circumstances –

  - The need for housing, to raise children or repay debts could all be relevant.

  - The relative wealth of the beneficiaries and the last known position of the missing person.

  - Any illness, disabilities or health issues, including addiction issues.

- (Un)Certainty of the missing persons situation: In the same vein as above, consider the prospects of the missing person's situation becoming more or less certain over the next few years in correlation to the beneficiaries' circumstances.

- The economic situation: In times of high inflation, the missing person's share could quickly lose value in real terms. Conversely, if interest rates are higher or property prices are increasing, their share could increase in value in the immediate future. If there is an economic downturn or a housing crisis, distribution sooner rather than later may be preferable.

(c) Practical Considerations

Whilst not the central consideration, personal representatives should consider the practicalities of retaining the missing person's share and postponing the completion of administration.

In the probate context, the majority of trusts will simply be the estate. The purpose of most estates is to enable the testator to pass on their assets to chosen people whom they wish to have the benefit of those assets, whether expressly by will or statutorily by the intestacy rules.

Practitioners may therefore argue that, in the circumstances of the particular case, the proposed distribution would give practical effect to the will trust. Practitioners should consider:

- If the will or a letter of wishes sheds light on the testator's views and if the beneficiaries who would benefit from the proposed distribution are in a similar position to the missing person. For example, if a £10,000 specific bequest is stated to be to help raise a child, if the proposed distribution to the now-carer of the child, practical effect may be given to the trust.

- In most cases, it is at least arguable the retention of the missing person's share by the personal representatives, potentially indefinitely, will nullify the purpose of the trust.

- Conversely, if the structure of the estate and the trusts therein are to preserve assets, as can often be the case for chattels, this could militate against distribution. Especially if, for example, chattels are small and easily stored.

- If the personal representatives are entitled to charge for estate administration, as legal representatives are, there is a risk the share will be diminished or even exhausted by professional fees.

(d) Administrative Inconvenience

It is inevitable some consideration will need to be given to the administrative inconvenience of the estate. This was a key focus of the decision of the High Court in *Re Vanstone* (2023, Bristol District Registry), which indicated a willingness to depart from the traditional wisdom expressed in *Re Green's Will Trusts* [1985] 3 All E.R. 455 that administrative difficulties and inconvenience to the executors should not be a primary consideration.

The decision in *Re Vanstone* illustrates that equity will be flexible and the Court may be willing to give consideration to administrative inconveniences and costs in the right circumstances:

- By a will and codicil, the Deceased's residuary estate was split into four unequal shares to be distributed between the Deceased's children. Following the death of one beneficiary, 10% of their residuary share was split equally between two of the Deceased's grandchildren, the defendants.

- Both defendants had been street homeless for many years, and were known to suffer from alcoholism and related health issues.

- A specialist probate search firm found evidence that at least one grandchild had been alive in the last five years through an entry on the Electoral Roll. Otherwise, they found no evidence of death or life. The search was inhibited by Covid-19: limited physical searches could be undertaken and some of the homeless and food bank charities in the local area were not operational.

- An application under the PDA 2013 was not appropriate due to the lack of knowledge of death or life. The executors sought a Benjamin Order to enable distribution of the estate on the footing the grandchildren had pre-deceased the Deceased.

The High Court made the Benjamin Order. It was held that, despite there being no probability of death, rather it being just one of many possibilities (a slimmer possibility at that), a Benjamin Order can be made in cases where there is simply a probability that the beneficiaries will never be traced and where further searches are impractical. In a departure from *Re Green's Will Trust*, weight was placed on the administrative difficulties faced by professional executors retaining a small sum of money for an uncertain, extended period and the erosion of that share by related fees.

Unfortunately for personal representatives faced with those trickier situations, the older authorities still carry precedence. However, *Re Vanstone* demonstrates the remit of Benjamin Orders is flexible and the role administrative difficulties will have, particularly in the case of modest estates.

Finally, it is important to note that Benjamin Orders will be the appropriate route where the death of the person is not a probability but a possibility and where the evidence of life or death is limited or inconclusive, regardless of the broader conceptual difficulties faced.

F. THE DIFFICULTY OF INTERNALLY CREATED TRUSTS

Wills often create several trusts themselves. The same analysis and considerations will apply, but specific consideration will need to be given to the following:

- The correct person to bring the application. The will may appoint separate trustees, and if so, they may need to make the application rather than the executors (depending on the wording and constitution of the trust).

- Whether the creation of the trust is contingent on the missing person being alive or whether it would persist in any event.

- The nature of the created trust. As outlined earlier, if the missing person is an absolute discretionary beneficiary of the internal trust, a Benjamin Order may not be needed to distribute.

Life Interest Trusts

Particular difficulty could be caused by the creation of life interests in property. In typical cases, the Deceased's real property will comprise the bulk of the estate, but what might the Court consider when the property is to be divided amongst a set of beneficiaries (known as remaindermen), with a life interest in possession for the missing person?

The first consideration is always the probabilities of the missing person being dead, traced or resurfacing. In that sense, a Benjamin application should be approached in exactly the same way. However, the difficulty will arise if the broader principles require consideration.

By their very nature, life interests postpone the inheritance of the beneficiaries for some time – the wait is often measured in decades. That is unlikely to be determinative of the matter, as retention of the property is fraught with difficulties.

The personal representatives could be under a duty to maintain the property at the expense of the estate, and there may not be any provision which allows the personal representatives to let the property or allow other beneficiaries to occupy it. The potential result is the property remains empty for decades and the personal representatives may well die whilst the property is preserved. Therefore, all the circumstances of the case, the practicalities and the administrative inconvenience will take on greater emphasis.

The difficulties will be apparent. It is obviously inconvenient for the personal representatives to maintain a property for any length of time. This will be especially difficult as the personal representatives cannot know how much of the estate they will need to retain to ensure their reasonable costs and expenses of maintaining the property can be met, with wider ramifications on general administration.

No Remainderman or Consequential Provision

A separate tricky situation is if the internally created trust bequests property to separate trustees to hold on trust for the missing person or they are to hold it on trust with an interest in possession for the missing person, without any consequential provision for if the missing person predeceased the Deceased. Whilst the intricacies of the correct person to bring an application in varying circumstances is beyond the scope of this work, it is likely the bequest will fail.

G. STEPS TO TAKE BEFORE MAKING AN APPLICATION

Once in a position where an application could be made, the personal representatives should consider the potential costs involved. As discussed earlier, insurance is the primary alternative step; it can be cheaper and more protective for the personal representatives. But if they are satisfied a Benjamin Order is needed and/or desired, the personal representatives will need to take a number of preparatory steps.

(a) Search Inquires

It is necessary to make enquiries into the whereabouts and status of the missing person. The below sets out the primary search inquiries. Is important to remember that not only are you looking for evidence of the missing person's life or death but of their circumstances.

It will be necessary in almost every case to engage a company which specialises in searching for missing people. There are a number of companies who conduct probate-specific searches. The search company will produce a report which usually forms the basis of the application and evidence in support.

Personal representatives must make their own inquiries. The personal representatives should ascertain from the friends and family of the missing person what information they know which may assist with searches or simply with the administration. The personal representatives should consider extending their searches and inquiries beyond those immediately known to them.

Online searches:

- Whilst it may be obvious, simply searching a person's name online or social media could produce the answer needed or set a train of inquiry in motion.

- There may be local or foreign news reports of the missing person, whether it be their death or something they have done.

- The missing person may have a social media account. If so, it would be prudent to attempt to contact them through that account. Their account may also provide evidence of death in more subtle ways. If the missing person was a frequent poster, active every day, then posts and engagement suddenly stopped, that point could be used as an indicator of a date of death.

Search the electoral register:

- This may produce results on the current or former addresses of the missing person. Past or present registration on the electoral register will create a train of inquiry which should be followed.

- Firstly, the missing person may still be living at that address. Secondly, if not, information could be obtained from the current occupiers or a landlord.

- If there are active addresses in the last seven years, particularly if there are multiple addresses, this may determine whether a Benjamin Order instead of a PDA 2013 application is required.

Make enquiries with police, charities, local authorities, or workplaces in the area in which they were known to have lived and worked.

There will need to be extensive and thorough searches – it is no light task to permit distribution on the basis someone is dead. However, the extent will vary depending on the estate and the missing person's share. Considering the situation in *Re Vanstone*, if the Defendants' share was £1 million each and the estate was valued at several more million pounds, the Court would have directed additional and more extensive searches be undertaken. Conversely, as was the case, the shares were relatively small and the estate modest in value.

(b) Consultation

The personal representatives should consult with the beneficiaries before, during and after the process. A Benjamin Order is necessarily an application which requires lesser consultation than other types of trust and estate applications. However, personal representatives must remember they are under a duty to keep the beneficiaries informed of matters affecting the estate and the administration. It is therefore incumbent on the personal representatives to:

- Inform the beneficiaries of the application and the reasons for it. As part of this exercise, the personal representatives should canvass the views and support of the beneficiaries. As a Benjamin Order will affect the beneficiaries – positive or negative – it is essential to ascertain their position. They may not wish to be burdened by liability for the missing person's share if they resurface or a beneficiary may be happy to take the risk and receive their distribution before legal expenses diminish it (in which case, the personal representatives should obtain an indemnity from the beneficiaries).

- The personal representatives should keep the beneficiaries updated with the progress of drafting the application.

- If the share is at risk of depletion whilst held by personal representatives, and the beneficiaries do not want to bear the risk of the missing person resurfacing, it may be that an application to pay the money into Court is more appropriate.

Linked to the above, the personal representatives will need to ascertain the likely costs of making an application early on. As will be addressed in greater detail in Chapter 9, the personal representatives will be able to recover their reasonably incurred costs and expenses from the estate. The Court can and usually will authorise a proportion of costs to be deducted from the share of the missing beneficiary, although a proportion of the costs will usually be borne by the estate. If costs are predicted to outweigh the missing beneficiaries' share, insurance will be preferable.

Once the personal representatives have assured themselves that a Benjamin Order is necessary, appropriate and have undertaken the preliminary steps, the next step is to draft the application.

H. Drafting the Application

An application for a Benjamin Order is made pursuant to the procedure in Parts 8 and 64 of the Civil Procedure Rules 1998. This requires:

- Part 8 Claim Form. This can be downloaded from gov.uk (Form N208). For those unfamiliar with litigation, a Particulars of Claim is not required. In more complex cases, it may be preferable to draft a separate Details of Claim to flag and present any difficult legal issues.

- Witness statement filed alongside the Claim Form.

(a) Claim Form

The Claim Form must:

- State that Part 8 applies. It should also state that Part 64 applies and the application is made pursuant to the principles in *Re Benjamin*.

- Contain a brief outline of the facts. The Claim Form is supported by a witness statement which will contain more detail, so only the core facts underlying the application need be stated.

- State the Court is being asked to approve the distribution of the estate on the footing that the missing person has died and/or that they otherwise died before a given date in certain circumstances.

- State the personal representatives act in that capacity. If the personal representatives are also beneficiaries, they will not be acting in their capacity as beneficiaries and should not state the claim is also brought in their personal capacities.

(b) Witness Statement

The witness statement should be given by the personal representatives. Generally, the witness statement will be drafted on behalf of the personal representatives by the solicitor with conduct of the matter and administration of the estate.

It is crucial to remember that the evidence will remain that of the personal representative. The statement of truth is signed by them or signed in their name, and they may be called upon to give oral evidence if the Court so requires.

The witness evidence should contain:

- The details of the Deceased and the estate, administration up to the point of the application, and any will or intestacy.

- Details of the missing person. For example, their relationship to the personal representatives, any health conditions, or any addictions.

- An explanation of the circumstances in which the person went missing, why they are suspected to be dead or why, if they are not suspected to be dead, they cannot be traced.

- Detail the efforts taken to investigate and locate the missing person, including efforts to confirm their death and life. The more detail the better.

- The consequences for the estate and beneficiaries if the proposed distribution is approved.

The witness statement should exhibit the documents which are referred to in the witness statement. All other relevant documents should be filed alongside the witness statement and claim form. This will include documents such as the probate search report, correspondence with police etc., and the results of any online searches. Don't forget the testamentary documents: the grant of probate and an up-to-date inventory and account.

(c) Parties to the Application

The parties to the claim will be:

- Claimant(s): The personal representatives – every personal representative should be a named claimant.

- Defendant(s): The missing person or persons.

- Unlike some claims involving trusts and estates, it is not necessary to add another representative beneficiary or beneficiaries.

The claim can legitimately be brought without naming a defendant, with "No Defendant" stated in the box on the claim form.

The claim form and witness statement should state "In the estate of Deceased (deceased)" above the names of the parties.

(d) Issuing

The application is to be issued in the Chancery Division of the High Court. For those outside of London and the South-East, the application should be filed at the relevant District Registry of the High Court.

The Court fee is per Fees Order 1.5 as a claim for something other than money or possessions. The civil Court fees can be found on gov.uk.

I. After Making the Application and Before the Hearing

(a) Representation of the Missing Person

The first consideration is whether the missing person should have a representative appointed by the Court to represent their interests. In most run-of-the-mill estates, even of large value, this will be unnecessary. Where the estate is significant, particularly if it involves intricate trust structures or company implications, it may be appropriate to apply for an order appointing a representative for the missing person.

The Court may also require a representative be appointed if there are doubts as to the personal representative's ability to independently act. For example, if a sole personal representative stands to benefit significantly from the grant of a Benjamin Order or they have demonstrated a lack of neutrality.

Such an application is made under CPR r.19.9. The procedure and requirements can be found in CPR 19 and Practice Direction 19, with helpful commentary in the White Book from 19.9.1.

The second consideration is if the missing person is a child:

- CPR Practice Direction 64B, paragraph 7.10 states the Court will expect to see the instructions to and advice of an appropriately qualified lawyer as to the benefits and disadvantages of the proposed and any other relevant course of action from the point of view of the child. It is doubtful that this provision could apply to Benjamin Applications; by their very nature the benefits and disadvantages are clear. Nevertheless, compliance may still be desirable to ensure the smooth progression and determination of the application.

- A litigation friend will in theory be required before any step apart from service of the claim form may be taken. The procedure for appointing a litigation friend with and without the need for a Court order is set out in CPR and Practice Direction 21. Naturally, as the person is missing, the claim form cannot be served. Therefore, the stage at which a litigation friend becomes necessary – after the service of the claim form – does not arise. In turn, a litigation friend would not strictly be necessary. The authors recommend the parents, carers or next of kin of the child are informed nonetheless (to the extent they are not already).

J. Preparation for the Hearing

The Court will include directions for filing bundles, skeleton arguments and arrangements for the hearing in the notice of hearing. The following are general pointers:

- A second witness statement will be required if there have been any developments. Minor points can be advanced by counsel in the hearing, but should any additional documentation require explanation or there is information regarding the whereabouts or life or death of the missing person, that is appropriate to be sworn by a statement of truth in a witness statement.

- For those unfamiliar with litigation, a bundle will need to be filed with Court a certain number of days before the hearing.

- A skeleton argument should be drafted to assist the Court.

- A schedule of costs should be drafted and filed. This should be limited to the costs attributable to the application. It can include disbursements such as probate search costs and time spent trying to trace information about the missing person. It should not include general estate administration work. Unless the Court directs a detailed assessment of costs, which is most unlikely, use Form N260 for summary assessment.

For any hearing in the High Court, only those with rights of audience – counsel or solicitors with the appropriate higher rights qualifications – may advocate in Court. Personal representatives can act on their own behalf as litigants in person.

K. THE HEARING

The first hearing is likely to be listed for at least two hours, plus time for judicial reading. The Court may list a preliminary hearing or a final hearing if the papers are in order. It will be heard by a Master in the High Court in London (sitting in the Rolls Building) or a District Judge or s.9 Circuit Judge in the District Registries.

The judge should be taken through the facts, law, investigations and varying possibilities. This work does not cover how to present an application, but there is nothing distinct or special about Benjamin Applications – they ought to be presented in the usual manner.

The judge may direct further inquiries or require advertisement. If satisfied with the evidence before them, the judge will make the order.

L. POST-HEARING

On the making of an order, the personal representatives are entitled to distribute the share in accordance with the Court's direction. It is advisable to wait until a sealed version of the order is in hand except in urgent applications, in case any immediate post-hearing issues arise (for example over wording, figures or dates).

It is vital the recipient beneficiaries are informed that a Benjamin Order does not relinquish or destroy the missing person's right to their share. Rather, it protects the personal representatives from liability. Should the missing person surface or it is proved they did not pre-decease the Deceased, the missing person or their estate can claim their share from the beneficiaries.

M. SUMMARY

The *Re Benjamin* jurisdiction is broad and exceptionally useful to enable estate administration when people have gone missing. The jurisdiction maintains a great deal of relevance post-PDA 2013, not least because of the flexibility it affords as an equitable rather than statutory process.

Distilled down, the key points to consider are:

- The Benjamin Order is appropriate where the evidence of life or death, or circumstances of either, are less than conclusive. But consider insurance as an alternative.

- The central consideration is whether the missing person is dead, can be traced or will reappear on the probable inference(s) from the facts of the case, but need not be premised on other circumstances being an impossibility.

- In all the circumstances, should the personal representatives be allowed to distribute and the beneficiaries allowed to enjoy their apparent interests now rather than later.

- Thorough searches and inquiries must be undertaken. The extent and scale will depend on the size of the estate and share, although it is better to be safe than sorry.

- Keep the beneficiaries informed.

PART THREE

OTHER MATTERS

CHAPTER EIGHT

MISCELLANEOUS SITUATIONS

There are a number of other situations which may involve missing persons outside the usual run of claims (themselves a relatively rare set of cases). These situations are not strictly confined to either Type 1 Cases or Type 2 Cases, albeit they will generally arise in Type 2 Cases. This chapter will consider:

- missing creditors;
- missing personal representatives;
- urgent situations;
- payment into Court; and
- Consular Provisions: Foreign Residents.

A. Missing Creditors

Personal representatives are under a duty to discharge any debts of the estate with due diligence having regard to the assets in their hands. Whilst "due diligence" does not have a global definition, the personal representatives are expected to satisfy debts as soon as possible and should do so within the executor's year.

The debts of the estate take priority over all other payments. This means personal representatives should prioritise investigating missing creditors or unascertained debts over payments to beneficiaries. This will feel unnatural to lay personal representatives, particularly in more modest, intra-family administrations. However, the personal representatives owe a duty to do so to both the creditors and beneficiaries. The personal representatives may find themselves personally liable in devastavit if the creditors or beneficiaries incur losses as a result.

(a) When is a creditor missing?

There are two contexts in which creditors can be described as missing: (i) where a known creditor cannot be traced, and (ii) when personal representatives believe the Deceased was indebted but cannot ascertain to whom that debt was owed.

(i) Creditors Cannot be Traced

Personal representatives should take the same investigatory steps to trace the creditor and information about the debt as for a Benjamin Order in respect of missing beneficiaries, with a need to consider the potential acquisition or insolvency of companies. Company and insolvency issues are beyond the scope of this work – if you are concerned a debt is owed to a company which may have been subsumed by another or has been wound up, contact a specialist company or insolvency practitioner.

(ii) Unascertained Creditors

The personal representatives may come across evidence the Deceased was indebted. For example, the will may refer to a debt being owed to "George", but George cannot be traced nor is there any information which would shed light on the debt. Other situations include incomplete reference in a ledger or a specific sum being set aside in a bank account labelled as debt repayment.

(b) Qualification of Duty

The duty to creditors is not so onerous that personal representatives are obliged to track down and contact every potential creditor. In *Re K* [2007] EWHC 622 (Ch), Richard Arnold QC, as he then was, sitting as a Deputy High Court Judge gave the following reasons why it may be inappropriate to notify potential creditors (at [25]).

> "First and foremost, notification carries the obvious risk of stirring up claimants who have been dormant for a long time (in some cases, for over 14 years), and who might easily misinterpret notification of the application as in some way constituting an invitation to proceed with their claims when they would otherwise not do so. Secondly, there would be practical difficulties in notifying all the Potential Creditors since the Administrators do not have current contact details for all of them and some appear to be abroad. Thirdly, even simple notification would involve the Administrators in expense."

Mr Arnold QC drew his judgment in large part from the decision in *Re Yorke* [1997] 4 All E.R. 907, in which Lindsay J stated at 922:

> "[The Court should] have it in mind to achieve a fair balance between, on the one side, the injustice of beneficiaries being kept out of benefit on account of liabilities that cannot be quantified and which may never come to anything and, on the other, the risk of the unknown and contingent creditors who have paid for cover finding their matured debts unmet."

Lindsay J went on to conclude the options open to personal representatives are: (1) retain funds; (2) obtain an indemnity from the beneficiaries; (3) obtain insurance; (4) seek the Court's sanction. The authors consider there are additional options, discussed below.

(c) Steps to Take

- Advertisement under s.27 TA 1925 is non-negotiable. This route is only possible in the second category – even then, only potentially. Section 27 does not afford protection if the personal representatives had notice of the claims (formal or informal). This step should be taken regardless, and promptly; five months post-death has been held to be late.[324]

- Retain sums sufficient to pay the debt, to be held on trust. Personal representatives should be wary of a potential claim for interest additional to the debt and consider a high interest account. In the case of large cash reserves or significant debts, this option may not be preferable for the personal representatives and could be unfairly prejudicial to beneficiaries.[325]
- Seek the sanction of the Court under the *Re Benjamin* principles and/or Part 64. This could be advanced on three fronts: (1) approval to pay the debt to the creditor's next of kin; (2) approval to distribute to the beneficiaries; (3) approval to not notify potential creditors. The Court is likely to expect an indemnity from the recipient.
- Obtain an insurance policy for the debt. There may be great difficulty obtaining such a policy as inevitably there will be a more limited search conducted compared to a missing beneficiary.
- Obtain an indemnity from the beneficiaries.
- Payment into Court (discussed in detail below). This is discouraged by the Court and should be a last resort.

B. MISSING PERSONAL REPRESENTATIVES

There is a finite number of situations in which a missing personal representative will cause issues. In the normal run of things, an application for a grant to the Court can be made by a beneficiary, other next of kin or person interested in the estate. In certain limited circumstances, if the executor is a foreign resident and cannot be traced

[324] *Re Kay* [1897] 2 Ch. 518 at 523

[325] As was held in *Ingrey v King* [2015] EWHC 2137 (Ch), in which a charge over property was deemed more appropriate

in that country, a consular officer can take a grant of representation in their place (see Section E below).

There may be some urgent situations when a special grant can be obtained, dealt with below. Otherwise, an application by others interested in the estate will be needed. Firstly, to appoint another personal representative to enable estate administration. Secondly, as in many cases they will also be beneficiaries, to begin investigations into their whereabouts and potentially apply for PDA 2013/Benjamin Orders.

C. Urgent Situations

Classic examples of an urgent situation include:

- Company decisions need to be taken for business protection reasons, to enable funds to be released from bank accounts or authorisation to be given for transactions.

- Real property is deteriorating and action is needed to prevent further damage or to take necessary steps to evict squatters.

- Consent is needed to finalise a property or investment transaction, failing which the estate may be liable for aborted sale costs (i.e. loss of deposit).

In such cases, it is appropriate to obtain a grant of probate ad colligenda bona, otherwise known as a preservation grant. It is not appropriate to use an ad colligenda bona grant to circumvent the normal process of probate, with all the delays that come with it.

An application should be treated in a similar way to a pre-action injunction and the procedure is largely the same. For a fuller explanation of the procedure, the reader is directed to *Williams, Mortimer & Sunnucks* [15-48]. It is worth noting that an application may be made and a grant ad colligenda bona can be obtained by a complete stranger, which means a non-beneficiary can obtain a grant if the personal representative cannot be traced or the beneficiaries are not willing or able to take a grant if a situation demands urgent action.

D. PAYMENT INTO COURT

The ability to pay estate money or securities into the Court is under s.63 of the TA 1925. Once the Court office provides a valid receipt, the personal representative will be discharged from liability going forwards. Payment into Court does not transfer or vitiate a personal representative's liability for acts or omissions up to that point and a personal claim can still be made against them for devastavit, for example.

In the case of smaller sums of money, it may be tempting for a personal representative to absolve responsibility or avoid spending estate money on a potentially expensive Benjamin application by payment into the Court. This course of action is highly discouraged by the Courts, particularly as there are a number of other options available to personal representatives. If payment into Court is made without a sufficient justification, for example because personal representatives simply cannot be bothered to investigate the whereabouts of a beneficiary, they may be liable for any additional costs caused by the payment into Court.[326]

If satisfied a payment into Court is the proper, it is usual and appropriate for the personal representative to deduct their reasonably incurred costs and expenses before payment. Those costs include the costs of payment into Court. *Lewin* at [39-117] advises that a witness statement in support of the application states the amount deducted and how that sum is calculated.

[326] See the comments of Eve J in *Re Salamons* [1920] 1 Ch. 290 at 297 in respect of the previous iteration of s.63 of the TA 1925

The application is made by Form CFO 103 in accordance with CPR Part 37 and the Court Funds Rules 2011.

E. CONSULAR PROVISIONS: FOREIGN RESIDENTS

The Consular Conventions Act 1949 has two (relevant) functions:

- section 1(1) enables a grant of representation of an estate to be made to a consular officer if a foreign national is named as an executor; and

- section 1(2) enables a personal representative to pay any share of an estate to a consular officer if the beneficiary is a foreign national of certain countries.

Those countries to which s.1 applies are set out in a plethora of individual Consular Conventions Orders; see https://www.legislation.gov.uk.

(a) Grants to Consular Officers

The first function provides those searching for a missing executor to seek to have one appointed. Section 1(1) is confined to foreign nationals named as executors under a will – it does not extend to intestacy.

On an application by a consular officer, the Court will grant a consular officer a grant of probate in the estate if the Court is satisfied the foreign national is not a resident in England and no application for a grant has been made by the foreign national's power of attorney.

The Court may postpone the making of a grant for as long as it considers appropriate having regard to the circumstances of the case. There is no authority or guidance on when the Court will do so, however it is envisaged the Court may direct initial or further attempts to notify the foreign national of their right to a grant or take further steps to trace the national.

A grant of probate is made to the consular officer via their official title and will vest in/transfer to their successors without the need for a fresh grant or application. Under s.6, the consular officer does not enjoy consular protection from suit arising from their administration of the estate. As stated, there is no authority and very limited information on consular administration. It is unclear when, if at all, a consular officer will be willing to take on such a burden, particularly in the absence of immunity from suit.

Whilst it is open to any person (in theory) to petition a consular officer to take a grant of probate, it is likely they will only do so in the most exceptional circumstances.

(b) Payment to Consular Officers

Conversely, it should be easier, although still not simple, for a personal representative to make a payment to a consular officer. This subsection (s.1(2)) applies where a foreign national:

> "(a) is entitled to payment or delivery of any money or property in respect of any interest in the estate of a deceased person, or vesting in possession on the death of any person, or is entitled to payment of any money becoming due on the death of any person; or
>
> (b) is a person to whom any money or property comprised in the estate of a deceased person may be paid or delivered in pursuance of any enactment, rule or regulation, whether passed or made before or after the commencement of this Act, authorising the payment or delivery of such money or property without representation to the estate of the deceased being granted."

This provision essentially encompasses all situations. Section 1(2) also requires that the foreign national is not a resident in England and the personal representatives know that no other person in England has express authorisation to receive the money or property.

If satisfied, the consular officer has the right and power to receive and give valid discharge for the money or property as if they were authorised by a power of attorney. Therefore, once receipt is given, the personal representatives will be discharged from liability.

This subsection has the potential to be useful for personal representatives when the missing person is a foreign national and last known to have resided in a country to which s.1 applies. There remains the issue that, by virtue of s.6, consular officers do not enjoy consular protection in relation to any acts done pursuant to s.1(2). The hesitancy should be less so than under s.1(1), though, as the scope for liability and claims following receipt is significantly less than taking a grant of probate.

CHAPTER NINE

COSTS

As a matter of broad generality, personal representatives can recover their reasonably incurred costs from the estate to the extent they are not recovered from someone else.[327] The costs and expenses are not, in the proceedings at least, incident to proceedings in the Court. Therefore, the Court cannot exercise its discretion to cap the amount of costs personal representatives may recover from the estate absent misconduct in the proceedings. That is not to say those expenses and costs cannot be challenged by the beneficiaries in separate proceedings.

Subject to that, at the conclusion of proceedings the Court will determine the question of costs if costs are sought otherwise than in accordance with the personal representatives' general indemnity. The three main types of application discussed in this book have slightly different positions:

1. PDA 2013: The standard order is the applicant(s)'s costs of the claim be raised and paid out of the estate of the Deceased.

2. G(MP)A 2017: A guardian is entitled to be reimbursed out of the missing person's property for reasonable expenses incurred in connection with the exercise of their functions as a guardian, and the Court may make a direction to that effect.[328] The Claim Form should seek, as part of the guardianship order, a direction that the applicant is entitled to their costs of the claim to be

[327] Trustee Act 2000, s.31; see also CPR r.46.3 and Practice Direction 46. For a detailed commentary, please see *Williams, Mortimer & Sunnucks,* Chapter 59

[328] G(MP) A 2017, s.9(1)-(2)

reimbursed. If this has not done, the applicant should invite the Court during the course of the hearing to make such an order.

3. Benjamin Orders: The Court can direct some or all of the costs of the application to be deducted from the missing person's share prior to distribution. It is, however, unlikely the costs of searches and inquiries will be deducted from the share and will be borne by the estate (or certain elements of the estate such as the residuary estate), as those costs can properly be described as administration expenses.

When seeking payment of costs in G(MP)A 2017 and Benjamin Order applications, a Schedule of Costs in Form N260 should be filed at least 24 hours prior to the hearing to enable the Court to summarily assess costs at the hearing and make the necessary directions. Failure to do so may result in the costs-element of the application being adjourned to a separate hearing or may result in the Court making no order as to costs.

MORE BOOKS BY LAW BRIEF PUBLISHING

A selection of our other titles available now:-

'A Practical Guide to Probation Breaches and Other Applications' by Mark Thomas
'A Practical Guide to Remarriage and Divorce' by Cordelia Williams & Claire Howard
'A Practical Guide to Privacy, Transparency, Reporting Restrictions and Closed Proceedings in the Court of Protection' by Laura Mannering
'Beaumont on Barristers – A Guide to Defending Disciplinary Proceedings (Second Edition)' by Marc Beaumont
'A Practical Guide to Payments for Environmental Services' by Ben Sharples
'A Practical Guide to the Law of Pregnancy and Maternity at Work' by Rebecca Thomas
'A Practical Guide to Redundancy – Second Edition' by Philip Hyland & Collette Moore
'A Practical Guide to International Issues for Scottish Family Lawyers' by Susie Mountain, Donna McKay, Ken MacDonald
'A Practical Guide to the Law on Deprivation of Liberty' by Ben Troke
'A Practical Guide to Rights over Airspace and Subsoil – Second Edition' by Daniel Gatty
'A Practical Guide to the Law in Relation to Inquests' by Ramya Nagesh
'A Practical Guide to the Construction and Rectification of Wills and Trust Instruments (Second Edition)' by Edward Hewitt
'A Practical Guide to Data Protection in Social Housing' by Clare Paterson
'A Practical Guide to Spousal Maintenance – Second Edition' by Liz Cowell
'A Practical Guide to International Parental Child Abduction Law (England and Wales)' by Dr Onyója Momoh
'A Practical Guide to Deprivation of British Citizenship' by Sean Ell
'A Practical Guide to Commercial Property Service Charges' by Rachel Garton
'A Practical Guide to Clinical Negligence – Third Edition' by Geoffrey Simpson-Scott (Geoff)
'A Practical Guide to the Rights of Grandparents in Children Proceedings – Second Edition' by Stuart Barlow

'The Electronic Communications Code: A Practical Guide – Second Edition' by Kerry Bretherton KC, James Castle, Mark Loveday
'A Practical Guide to the Independent School Standards – September 2023 Edition' by Sarah McKimm
'A Practical Guide to Estate Administration and Crypto Assets' by Richard Marshall
'A Practical Guide to Parental Alienation in Private and Public Law Children Cases' by Sam King QC & Frankie Shama
'Contested Heritage – Removing Art from Land and Historic Buildings' by Richard Harwood QC, Catherine Dobson, David Sawtell
'The Limits of Separate Legal Personality: When Those Running a Company Can Be Held Personally Liable for Losses Caused to Third Parties Outside of the Company' by Dr Mike Wilkinson
'A Practical Guide to Transgender Law' by Robin Moira White & Nicola Newbegin
'A Practical Guide to 'Stranded Spouses' in Family Law' by Mani Singh Basi
'A Practical Guide to Residential Freehold Conveyancing' by Lorraine Richardson
'A Practical Guide to Pensions on Divorce for Lawyers' by Bryan Scant
'A Practical Guide to Challenging Sham Marriage Allegations in Immigration Law' by Priya Solanki
'A Practical Guide to Digital Communications Evidence in Criminal Law' by Sam Willis
'A Practical Guide to Legal Rights in Scotland' by Sarah-Jane Macdonald
'A Practical Guide to New Build Conveyancing' by Paul Sams & Rebecca East
'A Practical Guide to Inherited Wealth on Divorce' by Hayley Trim
'A Practical Guide to Practice Direction 12J and Domestic Abuse in Private Law Children Proceedings' by Rebecca Cross & Malvika Jaganmohan
'A Practical Guide to Confiscation and Restraint' by Narita Bahra QC, John Carl Townsend, David Winch
'A Practical Guide to the Law of Forests in Scotland' by Philip Buchan
'A Practical Guide to Health and Medical Cases in Immigration Law' by Rebecca Chapman & Miranda Butler
'A Practical Guide to Bad Character Evidence for Criminal Practitioners by Aparna Rao
'A Practical Guide to Extradition Law post-Brexit' by Myles Grandison et al
'A Practical Guide to Hoarding and Mental Health for Housing Lawyers' by Rachel Coyle

'Stephens on Contractual Indemnities' by Richard Stephens
'A Practical Guide to the EU Succession Regulation' by Richard Frimston
'A Practical Guide to Solicitor and Client Costs – Second Edition' by Robin Dunne
'Constructive Dismissal – Practice Pointers and Principles' by Benjimin Burgher
'A Practical Guide to Religion and Belief Discrimination Claims in the Workplace' by Kashif Ali
'A Practical Guide to the Law of Medical Treatment Decisions' by Ben Troke
'Fundamental Dishonesty and QOCS in Personal Injury Proceedings: Law and Practice' by Jake Rowley
'A Practical Guide to the Law in Relation to School Exclusions' by Charlotte Hadfield & Alice de Coverley
'A Practical Guide to Divorce for the Silver Separators' by Karin Walker
'The Right to be Forgotten – The Law and Practical Issues' by Melissa Stock
'A Practical Guide to Planning Law and Rights of Way in National Parks, the Broads and AONBs' by James Maurici QC, James Neill et al
'A Practical Guide to Election Law' by Tom Tabori
'A Practical Guide to the Law in Relation to Surrogacy' by Andrew Powell
'A Practical Guide to Claims Arising from Fatal Accidents – Second Edition' by James Patience
'A Practical Guide to Asbestos Claims' by Jonathan Owen & Gareth McAloon
'A Practical Guide to Stamp Duty Land Tax in England and Northern Ireland' by Suzanne O'Hara
'A Practical Guide to the Law of Farming Partnerships' by Philip Whitcomb
'A Practical Guide to the Law of Unlawful Eviction and Harassment – Second Edition' by Stephanie Lovegrove
'A Practical Guide to Costs in Personal Injury Claims – Second Edition' by Matthew Hoe
'A Practical Guide to the General Data Protection Regulation (GDPR) – Second Edition' by Keith Markham
'A Practical Guide to Working with Litigants in Person and McKenzie Friends in Family Cases' by Stuart Barlow
'Protecting Unregistered Brands: A Practical Guide to the Law of Passing Off' by Lorna Brazell
'A Practical Guide to Secondary Liability and Joint Enterprise Post-Jogee' by Joanne Cecil & James Mehigan

'A Practical Guide to the Pre-Action RTA Claims Protocol for Personal Injury Lawyers' by Antonia Ford
'A Practical Guide to Neighbour Disputes and the Law' by Alexander Walsh
'A Practical Guide to Coercive Control for Legal Practitioners and Victims' by Rachel Horman
'A Practical Guide to the Law of Driverless Cars – Second Edition'
by Alex Glassbrook, Emma Northey & Scarlett Milligan
'A Practical Guide to TOLATA Claims' by Greg Williams
'A Practical Guide to Elderly Law – Second Edition' by Justin Patten
'A Practical Guide to Responding to Housing Disrepair and Unfitness Claims' by Iain Wightwick
'A Practical Guide to the Law of Bullying and Harassment in the Workplace' by Philip Hyland
'How to Be a Freelance Solicitor: A Practical Guide to the SRA-Regulated Freelance Solicitor Model' by Paul Bennett
'A Practical Guide to Prison Injury Claims' by Malcolm Johnson
'A Practical Guide to Advising Clients at the Police Station' by Colin Stephen McKeown-Beaumont
'A Practical Guide to Antisocial Behaviour Injunctions – Second Edition' by Iain Wightwick
'Practical Mediation: A Guide for Mediators, Advocates, Advisers, Lawyers, and Students in Civil, Commercial, Business, Property, Workplace, and Employment Cases' by Jonathan Dingle with John Sephton
'The Mini-Pupillage Workbook' by David Boyle
'A Practical Guide to Crofting Law' by Brian Inkster
'A Practical Guide to the Law of Domain Names and Cybersquatting' by Andrew Clemson
'A Practical Guide to the Law of Gender Pay Gap Reporting' by Harini Iyengar
'NHS Whistleblowing and the Law' by Joseph England
'Employment Law and the Gig Economy' by Nigel Mackay & Annie Powell
'A Practical Guide to Noise Induced Hearing Loss (NIHL) Claims' by Andrew Mckie, Ian Skeate, Gareth McAloon
'An Introduction to Beauty Negligence Claims – A Practical Guide for the Personal Injury Practitioner' by Greg Almond
'Intercompany Agreements for Transfer Pricing Compliance' by Paul Sutton
'Zen and the Art of Mediation' by Martin Plowman
'A Practical Guide to Adoption for Family Lawyers' by Graham Pegg

www.ingramcontent.com/pod-product-compliance
Ingram Content Group UK Ltd.
Pitfield, Milton Keynes, MK11 3LW, UK
UKHW020146290926
15471UKWH00004B/715

9 781918 241129